TALES FROM CLEMSON'S 1981 CHAMPIONSHIP SEASON

Ken Tysiac

SPORTS PUBLISHING L.L.C.

SportsPublishingLLC.com

ISBN: 1-59670-061-0

Publishers: Peter L. Bannon and Joseph J. Bannon Sr.
Senior managing editor: Susan M. Moyer
Acquisitions editor: John Humenik
Developmental editor: Travis W. Moran
Art director: K. Jeffrey Higgerson
Dust jacket design: Kenneth J. O'Brien
Interior layout: Kathryn R. Holleman
Photo editor: Erin Linden-Levy

Printed in the United States of America

Sports Publishing L.L.C.
804 North Neil Street
Champaign, IL 61820
Phone: 1-877-424-2665
Fax: 217-363-2073
SportsPublishingLLC.com

Library of Congress Cataloging-in-Publication Data

Tysiac, Ken.
  Tales from Clemson's 1981 championship season / Ken Tysiac.
    p. cm.
  ISBN 1-59670-061-0 (hardcover : alk. paper)
  1. Clemson University—Football—History. 2. Clemson Tigers (Football team)—History. I. Title.

GV958.C56T97 2006
796.332'630975723—dc22
                              2006013412

CONTENTS

FOREWORD

By Perry Tuttle

I was probably one of the players whom Coach Ford protected most in practice. I guess I'm either fragile or I faked that I was hurting a lot.

So I wore a yellow jersey that meant I could run and catch during practice, but no one could hit me. That makes practice fun when everybody else is getting tackled.

When we were not going through offensive drills, quarterback Homer Jordan and I were making up plays. He would say, "Tut, if I ever nod my head, just run to the corner."

In the Orange Bowl, the game was on the line, and we broke the huddle. Homer nodded his head as I was lining up. What flashed through my mind at that moment was, "He's coming to me. I don't think that's the play."

I wasn't sure what to do, and I had to make a decision in a second. Everybody has to work as a team, so part of me wondered if I should run the play called in the huddle. Part of me wondered, "Is he really going to throw it to me?"

I ran to the corner.

He took his drop, threw it to the corner, and I made the touchdown catch that landed me on the cover of *Sports Illustrated*. That was an incredible moment. That's what makes a team a team. You know one another well enough that it's just body language. There's not a word that has to be spoken. I love it.

In the weeks between the final regular-season game with South Carolina in 1981 and the Orange Bowl, our excitement grew. We watched other bowl games and knew ours was the one that would be

Wide receiver Perry Tuttle grew up idolizing Dallas Cowboys wide receiver Bob Hayes and wore No. 22, just like his hero.

featured that year. Even though the practices were hard work, that Christmas break was fun because we knew the magnitude of that game. It seemed like the team grew even closer as a family during that time.

One of the things I love about Clemson and its people is that we talk about the Clemson family, and it is just as real today as it was then. It was real before I went to Clemson, and it's still there. In that small town, Clemson offers education, athletics, and family. That's what Clemson is all about.

I remember after the Orange Bowl, Homer Jordan and Cliff Austin just lying there on the ground. We were in this world of our own, and we had done what we set out to accomplish, but what was important was that we experienced it with this group of great friends. That was cool.

I got a crazy call recently from Jeff Stockstill, who was my teammate at wide receiver. We make fun of each other, because that's just the way Jeff is. He's a nut. He kept everything alive. He's funny and a practical joker.

When we were done, he said, "Hey, Tut. I love you." And he hung up. You just don't find guys who say that. To me, Clemson University, the athletic department, and the Clemson family made that a part of what we do.

AUTHOR'S NOTE

Like many outside the Southeast, I had never heard of Clemson until it won the national championship in football in 1981, when I was 12 years old.

Growing up in Rochester, New York, I was a fan of the Buffalo Bills and enjoyed the NFL more than college football because I enjoyed watching teams throw the ball. I would pass my considerable free time during the holidays watching an occasional bowl game, though, and I was sitting at the kitchen table reading the morning newspaper on January 1, 1982, when my father walked in.

Ken Sr. has always been my best sports buddy, and I asked him what he knew about Clemson. I was reading about the Tigers, who were playing Nebraska in the Orange Bowl that evening. I had decided I wanted Clemson to win because it was nice to see a different team play for the national title instead of the usual powerhouses such as Oklahoma, Texas, and Southern California.

My father didn't know much about Clemson, either, but told me the Tigers were from the ACC, which is known more for great basketball than great football. I didn't care. I hoped Clemson would win anyway.

Though I had some inkling at that time that I would be interested in becoming a sports writer, I never imagined I would cover Clemson for a total of nine wonderful years with the *Anderson Independent-Mail* and *The (Columbia) State*. Or that I would marry a Clemson alumna, ensuring that my children would hear about Clemson at a much earlier age than I. Or that I would write a book about that colorful, rags-toriches team that helped Clemson get recognized in many households like mine throughout the nation.

I never would have imagined how wonderful the people at Clemson are, either, and they were instrumental in helping me write this book. Tim Bourret, the school's esteemed sports information director, helped me in every stage of this project, beginning with putting me in touch with John Humenik, the fine acquisitions editor at Sports Publishing LLC. John and Travis Moran, the editor who helped produce my previous book on the late, great Clemson broadcaster Jim Phillips, have been tremendously helpful throughout this project.

Perry Tuttle, the exquisitely well-spoken senior All-America wide receiver, was generous to provide an excellent foreword. The players, coaches, and others associated with the team were generous with their time, and almost all of them told me stories that made me laugh out loud, leaving no scarcity of material for a tremendous book. Those who helped me include: Angel Dostal, Tony Berryhill, Bill McLellan, Bill Smith, Billy Davis, Jeff Davis, Bob Paulling, Bubba Diggs, Byron Harder, Tim Childers, Larry Van Der Heyden, Terry Kinard, Chuck McSwain, Curley Hallman, Dan Benish, William Devane, Dora Scott, Danny Ford, Frank Magwood, Jerry Gaillard, Homer Jordan, James Farr, Jeff McCall, Les Herrin, Joe White, Kim Kelly, Lawson Holland, Nelson Stokley, Anthony Parete, Anthony Rose, Ray Brown, Chuck Reedy, Ricky Capps, and Steve Berlin.

I am grateful for Mike Persinger and Harry Pickett, my editors at *The Charlotte Observer*, for their support in allowing me to write this book and capture a time in Clemson's history that must not be forgotten. Another *Observer* colleague, columnist Scott Fowler, has written excellent books for Sports Publishing LLC on the Carolina Panthers and the North Carolina Tar Heels, and provided me with valuable advice on producing successful books.

My wife, Lura, was a trooper for putting up with my long hours on the phone and writing late at night—and for making sure there was always chocolate ice cream in the freezer to provide the late-night sugar high to keep me awake. My five-year-old daughter, Ashley, kept me informed on all the college football scores while I was writing, and Baby Ken III was always willing to share his toy train engines when I needed a break. Well, almost always—sharing isn't always easy when you're two years old.

None of this ever would have happened, though, if it weren't for my parents. My dad instilled the love of sports, though he probably regretted it when spending Saturday mornings in a cold ice rink during my hockey lessons from October to March in frigid Upstate New York. My mom patiently helped me read the sports section long before I was in kindergarten, encouraging my love of words, writing, and journalism.

It all resulted in an unusual career with strange hours for me, but it sure has been a lot of fun.

It was important for me to get this book written now, for the 25th anniversary of the national championship, because memories of that season are starting to fade as the years pass. I tried to focus more on the personalities and the fun anecdotes from that season than on play by play, because the details of the games aren't as important as the stories of the people who made the championship possible.

After covering Clemson football for almost 10 years, I have the utmost respect for the national championship team and what it means to folks on that campus. If this book can capture and preserve just a sliver of what made that team great, I will be grateful.

BEAR'S PROTEGE:
Danny Ford's Winning Wisdom

" Playing at Alabama and being at Alabama, we were expected to do that [win a national title]. I probably would have been very disappointed if we didn't achieve that. We were awfully lucky and good, too, to do it. Our football team was good and got better and better, and it was a pretty doggone good football team at the end of the year. They didn't luck into it. They beat everybody they played, and nobody could beat them. "

—Coach Danny Ford

While speaking to the Spartanburg Touchdown Club in the fall of 2005, coach Danny Ford told a joke that captured his personality to near perfection.

He said he had a bull on his farm that was getting up in age and wasn't showing much interest in the females in the pasture. So Ford went to the veterinarian and was given a pill to cure the problem.

Ford forced the pill down the bull's throat, and soon the bull had newfound energy. He chased the cows up and down hills and was more popular with the ladies than he'd been even as a younger stud.

"I don't know exactly how the pill works," Ford said. "But I know it tastes like peppermint."

The anecdote was vintage Danny Ford—funny, charming, and perhaps a bit risque. The only coach to lead Clemson to a national championship in football was born Danny Lee Ford in Gadsden, Alabama, on April 2, 1948. His father, Norris Ford, quit school before he reached fifth grade.

"He was a pretty smart man not to have any formal education," Danny Ford said.

Because his father didn't have one, Ford appreciated the value of a college education. Norris Ford taught Danny the value of hard work, laboring in a cotton mill, a steel mill, and finally for 37 years in a rubber mill before he retired from Goodyear. Ford's mother, Etta, stayed at home and raised the children, cooking three hot meals a day and cleaning while Norris earned the family's paycheck.

Danny Ford and his siblings worked hard around the house and delivering papers, but their father allowed them to slack off on their chores if they were playing sports. Ford's sister, Patricia, went on to play basketball, and brothers Bobby and Joe were successful baseball players.

Football was Danny's game. He became a first-team All-SEC selection as an offensive tackle at Alabama in 1969, when he served as team captain. There he played for legendary coach Paul "Bear" Bryant, who, with his houndstooth hat and hardened demeanor, won six national titles with the Crimson Tide and retired in 1982 as the winningest coach in college football history with 323 victories.

"He taught us everything about football we know," Ford said. "I just wish we'd remembered about half of what he taught us. I'd have been a lot better football coach, because he was the very best there was."

Ford said Bryant's philosophy was simple. He wanted players to be the very best they could be, and he believed in outworking people. Because Ford played at Alabama late in Bryant's tenure, the legendary coach had long since finished with the Xs and Os of coaching by that point. The Alabama assistant coaches did most of the actual coaching, and Bryant delegated authority and served more as a CEO.

Ford later dealt with his own assistant coaches in a similar fashion.

"Coach Ford let you coach your position," said wide receivers coach Lawson Holland. "You were held accountable for your position on and off the field. He always told us that he would handle the officials, and we were to coach our players. He certainly gave you the liberty to substitute."

Ford displayed that confidence in his assistants with an unusual routine on Mondays during football season. Ford spent Mondays driving to high schools throughout the Southeast, meeting with high school coaches and watching prospects practice.

That was partly because he believed in pulling his own weight in recruiting. On Thursdays after practice, many of his assistants scattered to the areas they recruited to watch games on Friday nights. After getting just a few hours of sleep, the coaches would hustle back to Clemson in time to coach the Tigers during games.

If the assistants were going to spend time recruiting on the road during the season, Ford would do it, too. He also wanted to leave his assistants time to craft a game plan.

"They were hard paid to come up with their own ideas, and pretty much that's how it works," Ford said. "I trusted them tremendously."

TROUBLES IN 1980

Ford almost didn't make it to 1981 at Clemson.

In 1980, his second season as Clemson's head coach, the Tigers were 5-5 after 10 games. The fans were restless, and there was talk that if Clemson lost in the finale to South Carolina, Ford would not return.

"A lot of people were saying Ford wasn't the right person for the job," said defensive tackle William Devane.

Joe White, who took over as Clemson's academic advisor in the 1981 season, has an unusual vantage point on the 1980 Tigers because he was on an opposing staff.

White was an assistant coach on the Virginia Tech staff when the Hokies visited Clemson in 1980. Hokies head coach Bill Dooley's 1980 staff, which also included soon-to-be Clemson defensive coordinator Tom Harper, was impressed watching film of the Tigers in preparation for the game.

"Golly, this team is unbelievable," White remembers thinking. "They were really good."

White believes the Tigers struggled to a 6-5 record because they couldn't settle on a quarterback. Though Homer Jordan started and provided the Tigers with a solid dual-threat, run-pass quarterback, Clemson also used dropback passer Mike Gasque off the bench. Neither completed 50 percent of his passes, and they combined for four touchdown passes and 13 interceptions.

The Tigers were in danger of losing at home in the fourth quarter against Virginia Tech. Down 13-7, the Hokies had the ball 2nd-and-goal inside the 1-yard line. Twice the Hokies thought they had scored. Twice the Tigers held. Virginia Tech settled for a field goal, and the Tigers won 13-10.

When Harper and White were interviewing for their jobs at Clemson after the season, they discussed their opportunities with excitement. Harper told White that he'd been watching film and thought the Tigers could be excellent both offensively and defensively. White said Jordan's solidifying of the quarterback position made a huge difference.

"We were even better than Tom and I thought we could be," White said. "The maturity of Homer Jordan, you had a guy on offense that was just outstanding. He did it on offense with a really good surrounding cast."

Ford's adherence to one of Bear Bryant's teachings probably increased the pressure on Ford in 1980. Bryant taught Ford that "We" win as a team, but "I" lose as a coach. That meant that a good coach gave credit to his players for victories and took personal responsibility for losses.

That is a good way to keep players' allegiance, but it can get a coach in a lot of trouble. After five losses, former coach Frank Howard visited Ford to discuss that philosophy.

"People might start to believe you," Ford said Howard told him worriedly.

SPRINGBOARD

Ford's remarkable buildup to the South Carolina game demonstrated that he was plenty capable of coaching a winning team.

He and equipment manager Len Gough had conspired to order orange pants for the team, and Ford used them to motivate the players, telling them that Clemson didn't lose in orange pants.

"The fans went ballistic," said defensive end Bill Smith. "We had orange shirts, orange pants, and orange helmets on, we were decked out from head to toe. It was amazing we didn't have orange shoes on."

South Carolina had Heisman Trophy winner George Rogers at tailback and finished 8-4 that season, but was no match for Clemson in that electric, orange-loving environment and lost 27-6.

"We needed something to springboard us into the next year," Devane said.

They got it, and they didn't lose again until 1982.

Tailback Chuck McSwain said Ford made one subtle but significant change heading into the 1981 season. In 1980, he demanded that, on the bus and in the locker room before the game, his players should be quiet. He wanted them focusing on their assignments and getting themselves mentally prepared to play.

"All that ended up doing was making everybody tense," McSwain said.

McSwain said Ford apologized to the players heading into 1981. He said he was going to give the players freedom to prepare the way they wanted before the games.

"He always had the radio going in the locker room," McSwain said. "People would be laughing and talking and carrying on, and it worked."

Ford came up with another idea for change during a meeting with some of his seniors in the summer following the 1980 season. The players told him that he had been so inconsistent with his moods and practice plan during the season that they simply hadn't known what to expect from day to day and week to week.

When they won, Ford was pleasant and so were practices. When they lost, Ford could be an ogre. Upon hearing that, Ford promised them that he would institute a consistent plan in August that they would follow through the entire season.

"I told them we'd practice two hours a day, and as long as they did their very best in two hours, we'd stop it in two hours if we could get everything done," Ford said. "And if we couldn't get it done, we would do it again. I was being more of the same person every day."

THE PRANKSTER

One part of Ford's personality that always remained consistent was his sense of humor.

Perhaps his best prank ever came at the expense of offensive line coach Larry Van Der Heyden, who was summoned for jury duty one year at the same time Clemson's clinic for high school coaches was scheduled.

Ford didn't want Van Der Heyden to miss the clinic, so he sent him to promotions director Allison Dalton, who had a connection in the Pickens County Court system. Ford wanted Dalton to get Van Der Heyden excused. Van Der Heyden didn't hear back from Dalton and thus assumed his excuse had been approved.

On the Friday of the coaches' clinic, two uniformed policemen showed up at Clemson's practice field. They walked right up to Van Der Heyden, who by this time had long forgotten the jury duty issue.

"You're under arrest," they told him. "You were supposed to report for jury duty."

Van Der Heyden panicked.

"I need to call Allison Dalton," he said. "He was supposed to take care of it."

"I'm sorry," the officers replied. "We've got to take you in."

Van Der Heyden tried in vain to get Ford's attention. He begged the officers to allow him to make a phone call to Dalton to straighten out the matter. They handcuffed him and placed him in the car.

Danny Ford was just 33 years old when he coached Clemson to the national title.

Then Ford approached the car, laughing. He had enlisted the policemen's help with the gag, and all the other members of the coaching staff knew about it.

"He's a real prankster," Van Der Heyden said.

Veteran television broadcaster Brent Musburger fell prey to a similar prank. Musburger got along well with Ford because of their shared interest in farming. One day when Musburger was in town, Ford let him borrow his pickup truck.

Then he got the campus police to pull over Musburger and accuse him of stealing Ford's truck. They told Musburger the truck had been reported stolen.

"Finally, they let him know that they were just messing with him," Van Der Heyden said. "We had a lot of fun."

IN THE CARDS

"Fun" wasn't the word to describe how Tim Childers felt when he saw Ford come through his front door on a day he had decided to play hooky from high school.

Unbeknownst to Childers, Ford, who was recruiting him, planned to visit him at school that day. When Ford arrived at school and was told Childers was sick, he decided to visit Childers at home.

Childers' parents were at work. He and some friends were deeply immersed in a poker game with nickels, dimes, and quarters when the doorbell rang. One of Childers' buddies got up to answer the door.

Imagine Childers' surprise when Ford came walking in behind his friend.

"He's 6 feet, 5 inches tall, so it's hard to miss him," Childers said. "Of course, my jaw dropped to the floor when I saw him."

Childers was despondent. He grew up a Clemson fan, and he figured he had blown his chances at playing for the school he had admired all his life. Sure enough, Ford lit into Childers right there in front of his friends, calling him all manner of names.

Nonetheless, Childers signed with Clemson and started at strong safety as a sophomore in 1981, another testament to Ford's ability as a recruiter.

Ford worked so hard at recruiting that his assistants never wanted to let him down. Clemson had nine full-time assistant coaches, and by October, each one had about 12 players he was still working in the hopes the players would join Clemson.

By that time, the players had heard from the assistant recruiting them so many times that they weren't impressed. That's when the assistants brought Ford into the picture.

"When you brought the head guy in, it's like bringing the president," said wide receivers coach Lawson Holland. "It's the head coach. He'd make a big difference."

During the season, Ford would have more than 100 prospects whom his assistants wanted him to call, and Holland can't remember having to ask twice for Ford to call a player.

DOING IT RIGHT

When Ford got those recruits to Clemson, he demanded their best.

One day during the preseason, the Tigers were scheduled to scrimmage at Memorial Stadium.

They went through warmups and stretched, and started the scrimmage, but play was ragged. Danny Ford blew his whistle.

"Forget this," quarterback Homer Jordan remembers Ford saying. "If we're going to do it this way, we'll start over."

They did, from the very beginning. Ford sent the players back to the locker room, where they were to get undressed. They sat around for about two hours (classes weren't in session yet), then got dressed and taped again and went back out on the field.

The message got through, loud and clear. This team was going to do things right at all costs.

"It was a long day, I promise you; and when we got back, guys had a little different attitude," said defensive end Bill Smith. "I'll never forget that day."

When the team returned to the field, Ford got the practice started on a good note. He told linebacker Jeff Davis that, unbeknownst to the players, he had placed a tape recorder in the locker room, and he knew everything they had said about him.

It wasn't true, of course, and they all laughed and had a superb practice after that.

That was Ford's way. He was tough on them, yet related to his players better than many coaches. He was just 33 years old, so he wasn't incredibly out of touch with the young guys on his team.

What impressed Smith the most was Ford's willingness to put his arm around a player and tell him how much he was appreciated.

"You could have fun with him, but you've got to respect him," Smith said. "If you messed up, he would discipline you. You didn't want to get in the doghouse with Coach Ford, but he could relate to us; you respected what he did and you loved to play for him."

Wide receiver Perry Tuttle remembers Ford for also recognizing the things he couldn't change. Tuttle had excellent hands and great speed and could break open a game in seconds, but he said he wasn't much of a blocker. As much as Ford probably wanted to discipline Tuttle for his failures in that area, he recognized Tuttle's limits and accepted them.

Other players with less talent weren't as lucky. Clemson didn't throw the ball often, so receivers were expected to be able to block. That wasn't an easy talent for wideout Frank Magwood to learn, because he had been a high school quarterback—but he picked it up quickly out of necessity.

"We were a running team, and we pounded the ball at the defense," Magwood said. "We had to block. By not being the most popular wide receiver or the fastest wide receiver, I had to do something to contribute, so I had to do my thing [as a blocker]."

VIEW FROM THE TOWER

For Tuttle, the brown stains he saw on quarterback Homer Jordan's facemask spoke to the intensity with which Ford often addressed the players.

Tuttle was coming to the sideline during a game, and Ford had pulled Jordan aside for some heartfelt discipline. Ford was chewing tobacco and screaming at Jordan at the same time, and the brown tobacco juice stained Jordan's mask and likely hit Jordan in the face.

"I just thought, 'Oh, gross,'" Tuttle said.

Players admired Danny Ford because he knew when to challenge them and when to put his arm around them.

Tuttle didn't always like Ford, because he was gruff and demanding. Still, Tuttle calls Ford a great coach and a good man. He appreciated that, after practice, Ford would put his arm around players coming off the field or in the dining hall in his plainspoken manner.

"He always talked about your momma and your daddy, and again, that was a very countrified dialect," Tuttle said. "He would say, 'You came from good mommas and good daddies,' and he said that to the whole team."

Tuttle's most lasting memory of Ford is seeing him surveying practices from his crow's-nest tower. Ford would watch from there while assistant coaches ran the team through drills.

From his lofty perch, Ford would spot exactly what somebody on the offensive line was doing wrong. Then, as though he had eyes in the back of his head, he would wheel around and bark at a linebacker who was making a mistake.

Tuttle compares Ford's ability to monitor his team from the tower to that of a mother who seems to have a sixth sense about when her children are misbehaving.

"He had this incredible way of seeing things that only later I understood," Tuttle said.

Ford also found unusual ways to make a point. One week before a big game, he had some unusual-looking fried meat brought in to the players.

He asked them to try it. Some people thought Ford was up to some kind of trick, and declined, but many ate it.

"They were pretty good, actually," said fullback Jeff McCall.

Ford asked them if they liked what they were eating. They said, sure, it tasted like chicken. Then he explained that he had given them what's called "mountain oysters"—cows' testicles.

This, of course, brought about bedlam.

"There were people falling on the floor, running out of the room, spitting," said wide receiver Jerry Gaillard. "It was pretty hilarious."

Ford's message?

"Don't ever say what you can't do or what you won't do," McCall said.

Ford's pregame talks were legendary. He had a way of backing players into a corner and challenging them that made them ready to beat down the locker-room door before the game.

He would single out a player who had a particularly challenging assignment. He would ask if the player's mother and father were going to be at the game.

"Yes, sir," the player would reply.

Ford would ask if the player's girlfriend and high school coach were going to be there.

"Yes, sir."

Ford would explain that the player was facing a tough opponent that day and might not be up to the task. Ford would tell the player that he could either embarrass himself in front of his parents and girlfriend and high school coach, or he could give himself and his loved ones a reason to be proud.

"The little challenges he gave those guys got them to respond," said wide receivers coach Lawson Holland.

Members of Ford's staff weren't immune to those challenges. Before each staff meeting, Clemson academic advisor Joe White wondered which member of the staff Ford was going to embarrass in front of everybody.

Two common targets were White and trainer Fred Hoover. Ford always wanted to know why a particular guy who was struggling in class might not be available for Saturday's game, or why another guy might be missing practice because of injury.

"From the time I came [to Clemson] to the time he left, he improved greatly in dealing with me in academics," White said. "I think as time went on and the rules changed, I think he gave me a lot more support."

Ford didn't always show it, but he was as nervous as his players on game day. During the team breakfast, he sat down at a table with place-kicker Bob Paulling, who had nerves of steel and a strong stomach. Paulling had no problem eating on game day, but Ford couldn't eat.

He would push his plate across the table to Paulling, who would devour the scrambled eggs and whatever else was put in front of him.

"I don't know how all that came about," Paulling said. "But I always sat close to Coach Ford. It might have been superstition on his part."

Ford had a significant effect on center Tony Berryhill's sense of time. If Berryhill has an appointment at 10 o'clock, he gets there 20 minutes early. That's because Ford never tolerated players who were late.

"One of the rules was if breakfast was at eight o'clock, then the doors would shut at eight," Berryhill said. "If the bus was leaving at 10:30, do not be trying to get on the bus at 10:30, because it was going to leave you at the hotel. You would find your own way to the game."

Berryhill said Ford was fair in the sense that if players did things right in drills the first time, he didn't force them to repeat their actions. If they did things wrong, punishment could be severe.

Off the field, violating one rule resulted in severe punishment.

"You didn't miss curfew," Berryhill said.

Defensive tackle Dan Benish and linebacker Danny Triplett found out what happened when curfew was missed. Clemson's players appreciated Ford's discipline, but also thought he sometimes went overboard with rules.

An 11 p.m. curfew on Saturdays following games was unpopular, Benish said. One night after a home game, Benish and Triplett tested the rule. They were out with some female friends when Benish suddenly realized what time it was.

Curfew was 10 minutes away, but they were enjoying themselves. They decided to stay out late. The next day, at the team meeting, Ford informed his players that two members of the team had decided they didn't have to abide by the team rules. Those two players were expected to show up at Memorial Stadium after the meeting in T-shirts, shorts, and running shoes.

Benish and Triplett did show up, and Ford informed them that their punishment would be running up and down every set of stairs in the stadium. It was a brutal task. They were tired already from staying out late, and it was a hot, humid day.

Triplett vomited, and Benish is pretty sure he did, too. But they decided that when they finished, they would sprint to the end zone where Ford was standing to make it appear as though the punishment was easy. Ford wasn't fooled.

"Well, was it worth it?" he said.

Both players looked him in the eye without hesitation.

"Hell, yeah," they said.

Ford shooed them away.

"I don't want to see you guys the rest of the day," he said.

LORD OF THE RING

In January of 2006, Ford went to the bank to fetch his national championship ring out of the safety deposit box where he keeps it.

Ford is a farmer who doesn't have much use for even the most meaningful rings and watches he won throughout his coaching career. He doesn't need flashy jewelry to tell anybody what he has accomplished.

But he was doing a speaking engagement and had been asked to bring the ring so the children there could see it. He complied, and when he held the ring he realized it didn't fit his ring finger anymore.

He wore it on his pinky finger instead.

"I know it looks funny there, but it shows how much fatter I've gotten," Ford said.

Aside from gaining a few pounds, Ford didn't change much in 25 years after coaching Clemson to the national title, but he believes Clemson has changed profoundly.

"It was a lot of textiles and a lot of agriculture that you don't have now," Ford said. "The school is headed in a different direction. ... We enjoyed it back then, and I'm sure the kids that are there now enjoy it now, and the people that support it do. I think our crowd was just a good fit."

Because Clemson and Ford's staff fit in so well, his departure from Clemson following the 1989 season created scars in the football program that, a generation later, are only just beginning to heal. He was forced to leave after publicly challenging then-university president Max Lennon because Lennon refused to build an athletic dorm for players.

Danny Ford's Xs and Os were simple—play great defense, don't turn the ball over, and make prodigious use of excellent kicking specialists.

NCAA sanctions for football followed in 1990, but they were limited in scope and did not cite or implicate Ford in any fashion. There are many who believe Clemson would have remained an elite football power had Ford not left.

"We'll never know, obviously," said defensive tackle Bill Smith, now a member of the school's board of trustees. "It's just unfortunate what happened. I don't know all the details of what happened. I think he could have pretty much finished his career there, had there not been the problems that there were—whatever they were. He had a great program going, and I kind of hated to see all that end, but obviously there were reasons why it did end."

Ford went on to coach from 1993-97 at Arkansas, leading the Razorbacks to the SEC title game in 1995, then retired to his farm in Pendleton, South Carolina.

What pleases him most is the success his players have achieved after football. He estimates that he has coached 1,500 players and worked with about 2,000 students, including all the managers and athletic trainers.

The 1981 team helped train leaders in law enforcement (Billy Davis), athletics administration (Mark Richardson), and even university trustee Smith.

"There are a couple of them I really feel that need some help and may not ever overcome the situations they're involved in right now," Ford said, "but I think 95 percent of them, 99 percent, 98 percent, are ... very successful."

Ford has kept the simple life that made him so popular with Clemson folk. Despite all the money he made coaching, he still changes his own oil on the farm.

He said you never realize how much you fit in somewhere until you leave and the people back home continue to embrace you.

"I was so young when I started, and they grew with me; and I really believe they were pulling hard for us to do well because we needed so much help," Ford said. "I'd never coached before and started at an early age and never had a track record. They wanted to be so good here at Clemson."

Ford said Clemson people were eager to win big because they never had. For decades, the man who built the foundation of the program, Frank Howard, took the Tigers on the road to SEC locations such as Auburn, Alabama, and Georgia for a paycheck, only to see Clemson get its teeth knocked in by those more wealthy schools.

Georgia Tech wouldn't consent to travel to Clemson for a game, so the Tigers played in Atlanta for a paycheck. Howard had success in the comparatively weak ACC, but Clemson people wanted to succeed on a national scale in football, the sport they loved.

Ford helped them do it. He said that having played in Alabama's program, he expected to win on that level. Bryant expected to be the best, and Ford carried those expectations with him to win a national title at Clemson.

"It had never been done at Clemson, and it may or may not ever be done again at Clemson," Ford said. "There are not many teams in the country that can win national championships or people that win national championships. There's just one a year, but I'd have been disappointed if we didn't do it because we were brought up to believe we could do it."

2

'THAT SPECIAL CHEMISTRY':
Danny Ford's Staff

« Coach Harper was a father figure and did a really good job of motivating not only his players but the coaches. The coaching staff that year did just an outstanding job on both sides of the ball, offensively and defensively. »

—Academic coordinator Joe White

igh school coaches used to flock to Danny Ford's annual coaches' clinic to learn from him and enjoy his sense of humor.

They would begin arriving Thursday, hold the clinic on Friday during practice, and watch Clemson scrimmage Saturday. On Thursday evening, Ford would gather the coaches for a pig roast and explain how he put together his staff.

"Nelson Stokley was a golf pro," he would say.

"Larry Van Der Heyden was selling insurance.

"The staff was fired at Duke, and then Lawson Holland was coaching high schools when I brought him over here.

"I called Tom Harper to see if he knew any defensive coordinators, and he proceeded to tell me how good he was."

The high school coaches loved hearing Ford joke about his staff, but there was no doubt it was a good one. Curley Hallman, Harper, Stokley, and Chuck Reedy had been or would later become Division I head coaches. They were tireless recruiters and hard workers, and their players respected them.

Once a week during the season, they gathered at the Holiday Inn in Clemson along with their families for dinner. Those dinners helped Ford build a family atmosphere in which everybody came together.

Offensive line coach Larry Van Der Heyden said the staff members trusted one another to work hard and enjoyed one another's company.

"You can't fool players," Van Der Heyden said. "I think they know when a staff gets along. They can feel it, and they can sense it. You've got to have that special chemistry—no matter what happens—to be successful, and I think you've got to be a little bit lucky to do what we did."

A 'VISIONARY' ATHLETICS DIRECTOR

Clemson athletics director Bill McLellan worked almost exclusively behind the scenes with the football program, but there is no doubt his contributions were vital to the national championship effort.

Many football coaches prefer to work for an athletics director who played or coached football. McLellan fit that profile for Ford.

He grew up a short distance from the South of the Border tourist haven at the North Carolina-South Carolina line in Dillon, South Carolina, and began playing football as a center in eighth grade. In January of 1950, his senior year, he was invited to Clemson for a tryout, which was not prohibited by NCAA rules at the time.

Coach Frank Howard offered him a scholarship, and McLellan figured that was better than the deal Davidson offered him. McLellan said Davidson told him its scholarships were tied to academic performance. He said only the "A" students received full scholarships.

"My grades weren't all that good," McLellan joked. "I would have had to pay more for school than it would have cost for tuition."

Danny Ford was well known for hiring good assistants and allowing them to coach their positions the way they wanted.

McLellan earned two football letters and became athletics director in 1971 after spending 13 years in Clemson's athletics administration. He was instrumental in building first-class facilities for Clemson. During his tenure, the Jervey Athletic Center office complex was constructed, and Memorial Stadium underwent numerous renovations. He was among the first to create luxury boxes at a college stadium, and his addition of the upper decks at Clemson made the stadium a model for other schools for years.

"I thought he was crazy," Ford said. "That's just more people you have to please. But he had great foresight and was able to build the stadium and the two upper decks and pay for it. He just had great vision. The interest rate was awful high back then, but he found a way to do it. There were a lot of things that came together."

Current Clemson athletics director Terry Don Phillips has said McLellan's attention to facilities was so forward thinking that Phillips labels him a "visionary."

Hiring Ford proved to be one of McLellan's best moves. McLellan was surprised when Charley Pell left for Florida following the 1978 regular season. Thirty minutes before Pell got on the plane at the Greenville-Spartanburg Airport to leave for Florida, he told McLellan he was staying at Clemson. When that didn't happen, Ford became Plan B.

Though McLellan recognized that Ford was young and needed to develop organizational skills, Ford had enough positive traits to merit the job. Ford had played under Bear Bryant at Alabama, and Clemson rarely hired a football coach who didn't have Alabama roots.

Ford also had the people skills to be an excellent recruiter and a strong work ethic.

"Danny, he got in here and got to work like an old plow boy," McLellan said. "He got down on everybody else's level. He was a hard worker and knew how to relate to the players' families in recruiting."

McLellan believed in hiring good head coaches and letting them run their programs and hire their own assistants. That worked perfectly for Ford because he was hard working and hired a great staff.

Ford rewarded McLellan's faith with wins—but not right away. Many members of Ford's coaching staff believe they would have been fired in 1980 had the Tigers not defeated South Carolina to finish 6-5. McLellan said that's not true.

"It wasn't even close," McLellan said. "From where I was sitting, I didn't have any problem with [Ford]."

Joe White, the team's academic advisor, said McLellan, although he doesn't get much credit, was an essential component in that national championship season. White said McLellan always followed through on his promises and worked hard to build a family atmosphere.

"He did an awesome job," White said. "If you look at his accomplishments while he was here, you'd have to say he was a great AD."

Clemson's coaches called McLellan "Dollar Bill" because he was a brilliant money manager. He asked the canteen at the bookstore to handle concessions at the stadium, and the proceeds helped pay for scholarships. A Clemson trustee owned a rock quarry, and he helped with materials when the school needed to pave parking lots. The school's physical plant did a lot of the stadium renovations.

McLellan personally studied traffic patterns at length in order to help find the best way to get fans quickly and comfortably to and from games. Clemson defensive backs coach Curley Hallman, who later was head coach under McLellan at Southern Mississippi, remembers watching him there, smoking a cigar, watching the cars and thinking of ways to improve the flow of vehicles.

At Clemson, McLellan had done the same thing. A highway patrolman told him that, near the Armory off South Carolina-Route 76, traffic would flow a lot easier if he just cut down two trees. McLellan said his wife, Ann, was upset that the two oaks had to be cut down, but she got over it. Clemson's coaches were amazed that an athletics director would immerse himself in such small details.

Hallman, who calls him "Mr. Mack," said McLellan was the best athletics director with whom he has ever been associated. Hallman said McLellan probably could run an athletics department even today better than many of those currently in the business.

"He could milk it down now, and find ways to save money and find ways to make money," Hallman said. "He wasn't there to please everyone. He was there to take care of No. 1. And No. 1 was that athletic department, making money and giving you what you needed to be successful."

MAKING THEM STRONG

McLellan had a vision for Clemson's weight room at the Jervey Athletic Center. He wanted it to be the finest in the United States, and in 1976, he hired the late George Dostal to build it.

A high school coach in Ohio before he came to Clemson, Dostal had a Ph.D. in exercise physiology, and was a master motivator. McLellan gave him a blank check and told him to get to work building a weight room for the athletic program. McLellan wanted the best equipment Dostal could find.

Dostal built a state-of-the-art weight room and used some methods that were unorthodox at the time. He was far ahead of his contemporaries with his emphasis on stretching, and his cross training ideas included having William Perry jump off a diving board to improve his flexibility.

Heading into the 1981 season, Dostal was the first to suggest that the Tigers could play in the Orange Bowl. He put up posters saying Clemson's goal was to play in the bowl game that wound up deciding the national championship.

"He said, 'I believe it, and you've got to believe it, too,'" said quarterback Homer Jordan.

After Dostal proved prophetic, and the Tigers received an Orange Bowl invitation, Clemson's players got off the bus alongside Nebraska's players at a pre-bowl function. One of the Nebraska assistant coaches began teasing Dostal, saying his players were too tall and skinny.

"Well, yours are awful short and fat," Dostal replied. "And I don't think they'll move very fast on the field."

Clemson's stamina and conditioning made a difference in the Orange Bowl on a warm, humid evening in south Florida. A day afterward, Dostal was standing near a huge pile of shrimp at the post-bowl banquet when Nebraska coach Tom Osborne approached.

"I want to congratulate you," Dostal's widow, Angel, recalled Osborne saying. "I've never played against a team that had players in such good condition. You deserve all the credit for what happened here."

Dostal went on to work four years for the Atlanta Falcons before going off on his own to do consulting work. He never got the satisfaction working with the pros that he did with Clemson, and he died January 21, 2005.

His love for the 1981 team never waned.

"There is something very special about this group of kids," Dostal told his wife before that season. "I know they are going to do things they don't know they can do. I'm going to make sure they are strong enough."

TOM HARPER: KEY ADDITION

Some players feared the worst when they learned Clemson was hiring the late Tom Harper as defensive coordinator and defensive line coach heading into the 1981 season. They were afraid the white-haired Harper's age (he was 49) would prevent him from relating to the players on a staff whose coaches mostly were much younger.

They were pleasantly surprised. Harper was mature and relaxed and proved the perfect complement to Ford, who was younger and incredibly intense.

"His demeanor was so calm and so relaxed, and his work was mostly done behind the scenes, with films, with game plans, things like that," said strong safety Tim Childers. " ... I don't ever remember seeing him get emotional. He was always calm, cool and collected. I think he was a good fit for that team because we had such good leaders."

The players on defense didn't need inspiration—Jeff Davis, Terry Kinard, and Jeff Bryant provided plenty. They needed a teacher who would present them with a plan they could implement.

At times, they needed somebody to be their advocate, as well. Defensive tackle Dan Benish remembers one practice on a hot day when Ford seemed determined to wear out everyone with brutal hitting and conditioning.

Harper called the defensive linemen over and told them to take a knee in front of him. As was his custom as a chain smoker, he held a cigarette between the thumb and forefinger of his right hand. He knew Ford wouldn't challenge him as he gave the defensive linemen a break. He told the players to make it look as though they were meeting about something important.

Ford was with the offensive linemen, urging them on. He was encouraging the linebackers to work harder.

"Look at Coach Ford over there," Benish remembers Harper saying. "He's too afraid to come over and ask us what we were doing because he is afraid of the answer."

All the coaches on Ford's staff were treated with respect and allowed to coach their positions as they saw fit. Harper received the most latitude, though, because of his experience.

Defensive coordinator Tom Harper, center, brought much needed experience when he left Virginia Tech to join the Clemson staff before the 1981 season.

"Probably the smartest thing Danny ever did was hire Tom," said running backs coach Chuck Reedy. "Tom brought maturity. He brought a steadying influence to the staff."

WILLIE ANDERSON: IMPACT BEYOND FOOTBALL

Willie Anderson, who coached defensive linemen along with Tom Harper, saw a fight between teammates break out in practice one day.

The defensive line was doing a drill during which the young players were performing scout team-type duties, playing as offensive linemen so the starting defensive linemen could practice their techniques.

Steve Berlin, a lowly freshman at the time, was matched with junior Dan Benish for the drill. Berlin was trying to make a name for himself, playing too aggressively for the "dummy" looks he was supposed to be giving to benefit Benish. Berlin was fighting and scratching when he should have been offering token resistance.

Benish, enraged, attacked Berlin, throwing uppercuts. He grabbed Berlin's helmet and was either trying to tear the helmet off Berlin's head or Berlin's head off his body. Berlin was doubled over, trying to prevent Benish from hurting him. Rather than breaking up the fight, Anderson encouraged the overmatched player, Berlin, to fight back.

"You're not going to let him hit you, son," Anderson said. "Don't let him just hit you."

After Berlin stood up for himself a bit, the fighting ceased.

Like the rest of the coaches on Clemson's staff, Anderson insisted on toughness from his players, but he also was a player favorite for the way he cared about them. Anderson earned three letters as a middle guard at Clemson in the early 1970s, captaining the 1974 team that finished 7-4 under Red Parker.

Anderson played at Mayewood High in tiny Mayesville, South Carolina, and recruited free safety Terry Kinard and cornerback Anthony Rose from nearby Sumter.

Kinard often talks about the impact Anderson had on him. After playing seven years in the NFL, Kinard still didn't have his college degree. Anderson was defensive coordinator at Langston University in Oklahoma and invited Kinard to coach defensive backs there and continue his education. Kinard spent five years there and earned his degree.

"I don't think it was just because he recruited me to come to school," Kinard said. "He was more than just a football coach to me and I'm sure many other guys on the team. He made sure you took care of the things you needed to take care of, and he made sure you were taken care of."

HALLMAN'S "DAILY MUSTS"

Curley Hallman had been at Clemson two years when he turned down opportunities to coach at Texas A&M and Georgia before the 1981 season.

A Greenville sports reporter asked Hallman why he didn't take the other jobs. Hallman told him Clemson had good players returning and was a special place where a national championship was possible.

The reporter wrote a story making light of Hallman's claim, but Hallman had the last laugh. He also was a key reason the Tigers intercepted 23 passes and allowed just six touchdown passes in 1981.

After a short NFL career, Clemson safety Billy Davis called Hallman to tell him he was the best coach he'd ever had.

Hallman had been a three-year letterman at defensive back at Texas A&M, where he also lettered a year as a basketball player, so he understood the all-important footwork fundamentals he was teaching to the players in the secondary.

"He was a great motivator, knew what he was doing, really took care of the players. I loved playing for him," Davis said.

Hallman had coached linebackers the previous two seasons, but moved over to the secondary after Mickey Andrews left. His belief in fundamentals was reflected in his "daily musts"—drills to improve footwork and tackling techniques that had to be completed every practice.

Hallman was hard on his players, but also tried to be honest and kind. When he saw that players would rotate at every position except free safety, he called backup free safety Davis in to explain that he was a good player stuck behind an incredibly talented starter in Kinard.

Visiting strong safety Tim Childers' apartment one hot summer day, Hallman noticed that the air conditioning wasn't working, and it was unbelievably hot. Hallman had an old fan back at his house, and brought it for Childers to use. Childers promised to get it back to Hallman.

"When we had that 20th reunion, I said, 'Tim, where is my fan?'" Hallman said.

Davis said it was a great loss to him personally when Hallman left for another opportunity with his alma mater (Texas A&M) under Jackie

Sherrill immediately after the 1981 season. Hallman admits he experienced pangs of regret after leaving. He stopped at a convenience store payphone in Tyler, Texas, and called June Roach, Danny Ford's secretary.

Hallman said he needed to talk to Ford right away, but he was out of the office recruiting. Hallman was calling to tell Ford he wanted to come back to Clemson, but he never got the chance.

"So I got in the car, went to the motel, got organized, got recruiting, and said, 'Get on with your life.'"

Hallman's replacement in 1982 was Don Denning, who was Clemson's administrative assistant in 1981. Hallman was partly responsible for bringing Denning to Clemson because he had coached with Denning at Memphis State.

Denning had ties to South Carolina because he had played at Presbyterian College in Clinton, South Carolina. After leaving Presbyterian, he served as a second lieutenant in the U.S. Army for two years, and his temperament betrayed his military background.

"He was a high-intensified human being now," Hallman said.

Hallman usually shied away from hot-tempered coaches, but considered Denning so knowledgeable that Clemson couldn't afford to pass up an opportunity to hire him. Denning had been defensive coordinator at Western Carolina when Les Herrin, who coached Clemson's linebackers in 1981, was team captain there in the early 1970s.

"He was a worker," Herrin said. "An endless, tireless worker."

With Denning's help, five Memphis State defensive backs were selected in the NFL draft from 1975-80. Keith Simpson, made the ninth overall selection by the Seattle Seahawks in 1978, was among them. Hallman told Ford that Denning would be an asset whether he served as administrative assistant or coached on the field some day. As it turned out, Denning did both.

LES HERRIN:
HIGH SCHOOL TO HIGH TIMES

After the Orange Bowl, linebackers coach Les Herrin's mother told him that NBC's broadcast showed him in the press box during the game.

She asked him if he said, "Hi, Mom," when the camera focused on him.

He isn't sure he did, but he wasn't going to tell her otherwise.

"That's what she thought," Herrin said, "and I was going to keep it that way."

Herrin was in his first year coaching at Clemson and was in charge of weak side linebacker Jeff Davis and Danny Triplett, who shared time with Johnny Rembert at strong side linebacker. His coaching philosophy was to get players to do what he called "elevating" themselves. He said if you imagine a ladder where their ability was one rung, he wanted them to play a rung higher.

If they had average talent, he wanted them to become good players. If they had good talent, he wanted them to become very good players.

"If you're running a 4.6 [in the 40-yard dash], are you playing at a 4.6 or a 4.8?" Herrin said. "Do more film study, if that's what it takes. But play up to your ability."

Looking back, Herrin marvels at his good fortune from the 1981 season. He was 33 that year and relatively inexperienced in college coaching. He had served one year as Appalachian State's defensive coordinator after three years as coach at Central Davidson High in Lexington, North Carolina.

Defensive backs coach Curley Hallman said Clemson's coaches had been impressed with Herrin when they heard him speak at clinics.

The coaches also knew him because they had signed defensive end Edgar Pickett out of Central Davidson before Herrin left for Western Carolina. Offensive tackles coach Buddy King had recruited Herrin's area, and Herrin asked him if he might have a shot at a job on the staff.

"He was very knowledgeable and had a great relationship with the players," Hallman said. "He was really close to them and was going to make sure they did the things they were supposed to do—but those players, they could sense that they were important to him."

Herrin remembers being excited as he interviewed with Tom Harper, the new defensive coordinator.

"Do you want the job?" Harper asked.

"Yes, I do," Herrin replied.

"Well, you've got it."

Herrin went on to coach 14 years—half his career—at Clemson. He survived two coaching changes, staying on the staff to coach under Ken Hatfield and Tommy West.

He treasures a few special memories of that season. While Clemson was in Miami preparing for the Orange Bowl, Perry Tuttle and Jeff Davis were with Herrin's six-year-old son, Deke, when he was interviewed by TV anchor Stan Olenik.

Herrin laughs when he remembers sitting in the locker room before the Orange Bowl when Danny Ford walked in, wide-eyed, after pregame warmups.

"Did you see those big offensive linemen [for Nebraska]?" Ford asked. "They can run, too."

After growing up in the last house at the end of a dirt road in Waycross, Georgia, Herrin was living a dream. He said he didn't realize just how fortunate he was until years later.

"It was unbelievable," Herrin said. "I had been a high school coach at a small school two years prior to that. All of a sudden I was sitting in a press box on national TV in the Orange Bowl, playing for the national championship."

STOKLEY LAID DOWN THE LAW

Nelson Stokley's life would have been vastly different if the late coach Charles McLendon hadn't invited him to help out at spring practice following Stokley's senior season at LSU.

Stokley was planning to go to law school after a decorated career as quarterback at LSU, where he earned All-SEC honors as a senior in 1967. When Stokley tried coaching, he was hooked, and McLendon later invited him to coach full time.

"I really enjoyed helping those guys perform," said Stokley, Clemson's offensive coordinator and quarterbacks coach in 1981. "And then I knew that's what I wanted to do."

It's often said that good players don't often turn into great coaches, but Clemson's 1981 staff challenges that concept. Ford was an All-SEC lineman at Alabama, and Hallman played football and basketball in college.

Offensive line coach Larry Van Der Heyden was an All-Big Eight selection at Iowa State. Stokley might have had the best collegiate career of any coach on the staff, as he set numerous passing and total offense records at LSU.

Stokley's first-hand understanding of the split-second decisions required of quarterbacks made him an excellent position coach. His players were well drilled on the intricacies of reading and running the option. They read through their progressions and checks smoothly when they were passing.

Athletics director Bill McLellan said Stokley had an uncanny knack of making subtle changes in Clemson's schemes to fit the unique talents of each quarterback he coached. Stokley was a master at fostering the mental toughness and aptitude a quarterback needs to succeed.

"You handle the quarterbacks a little differently," Van Der Heyden said. "You've got to make sure that guy is confident in what he is doing. Linemen you can get on a little bit harder. He had a great way of handling the quarterbacks. He was very positive with them; he was well respected, and they really liked him and played hard for him."

Stokley's favorite call from the championship season came in the Orange Bowl. Clemson faced third-and-4 from the Nebraska 9 and lined up in a spread formation it hadn't used all season. Stokley said the television announcers were in the coaches' booth and expressed surprise at the call.

It was a quarterback draw, and their opinion was that it wouldn't work so close to the goal line. Clemson ran it anyway. Homer Jordan gained four yards, and Cliff Austin scored on a sweep two plays later.

Stokley went on to become a head coach at Louisiana Lafayette, where he enjoyed one of the most rewarding experiences of his life. His son, Brandon, played wide receiver for him and blossomed into an outstanding player in front of his eyes.

"As a coach, you don't get an opportunity to be with your family a lot, so it was really nice," Stokley said. "We kind of bonded together there, that's what I really got out of it, being around him and watching him develop and seeing what kind of football player and competitor he was. It was a lot of fun to me."

Brandon Stokley's successful career at Louisiana Lafayette landed him in the NFL, where he became one of Peyton Manning's favorite targets with the Indianapolis Colts. In his young career, he's already tallied nearly 200 receptions, 2800 yards, and over 20 touchdowns.

He was just five years old when Clemson won the national title, but even then people around him thought he might be headed for an athletic career.

"I don't think I've ever been around anybody's son that's all boy any more than Brandon Stokley," said Joe White, the team's academic advisor. "You just knew that, if he ever wanted to participate in a sport, he was going to be good, and to think he's done what he's done has just been great."

LARRY VAN DER HEYDEN: REDEFINES INTENSITY

Steve Berlin played defensive end but was close with offensive line coach Larry Van Der Heyden because the coach had played with Berlin's father, Ralph, at Iowa State.

Van Der Heyden still looked as though he could play when he was coaching at Clemson.

"I can remember getting my first look at him out there [on the practice field]," Berlin said. "He had these really short socks on, and his calves looked like big old cantaloupes on his legs, and this is a guy in his early 40s, maybe. He was in great shape."

Van Der Heyden worked out at noon each day to relieve stress. He often would leave the office puzzled over how to make a particular blocking scheme work, only to realize the answer while he was running or lifting weights.

"All of us linemen would wonder if Coach Van Der Heyden had run before practice," said starting left offensive guard James Farr. "He was always a little calmer if he had run before practice. We knew we would be in trouble if he hadn't run before practice. We'd always talk about that."

Berlin calls Van Der Heyden the most intense coach he has ever met. He would go wild with anger when one of his linemen made a mistake, which prompted Berlin's lasting memories of Van Der Heyden's cap.

During an especially heated and hot late summer practice, Berlin glanced at the bill of Van Der Heyden's cap, which was soaked all the way through with sweat that was dripping off the bill. At that moment, Berlin thought to himself that there would never be another coach like Van Der Heyden.

Van Der Heyden and fellow offensive line coach Buddy King had the most difficult jobs on the staff because Ford's specialty was offensive line, and he was demanding of his linemen. Van Der Heyden said Ford was known for letting his assistants do their own thing, but kept a special eye on the offensive line.

"He was probably a little more critical of that position than some of the others because he'd coached it, and if things weren't done right, he would see it," Van Der Heyden said. "Some other head coach, if they were a quarterbacks coach, they would probably miss something. But because he was a line coach, he didn't miss it."

Van Der Heyden said he was comfortable with Ford even though it's an unwritten rule in coaching that it's not good to work for a coach whose specialty is your position. That might be because Van Der Heyden's intensity matched Ford's. Van Der Heyden believed he needed to coach the way his players should play, and that meant conveying demands with intensity, shouts, and screams. He also was an effective teacher. Few groups of teammates in sports have more complicated teamwork tasks than offensive linemen, and Van Der Heyden did an excellent job making sure they knew their assignments.

Every Friday afternoon before a game, he tested his players.

"Coach Van Der Heyden would pull out sheets with different defensive formations," said center Tony Berryhill. "He'd have a play called, and you'd have to draw your block on the piece of paper to make sure you knew your plays."

It was no accident that Clemson's offensive line provided excellent protection for Jordan.

Van Der Heyden was a stickler for precision, beginning with the huddle break. Everybody broke the huddle and ran to the line of scrimmage. On the snap of the ball, every lineman's hand was to come off the ground at precisely the same time.

Van Der Heyden demanded that his players stay low, step with the correct foot, and play until the whistle blew. The players on the 1981 team were experienced enough to know that Jordan could make big plays if they protected him—and hustled.

"We realized that if everyone did their job, then the play would be successful," Berryhill said. "The cut blocks. The slant picks. The hustle. Getting downfield. It was all there."

Van Der Heyden shared responsibilities with King, who coached the tackles while Van Der Heyden handled the centers and guards. Theirs was a good working relationship because they welcomed input from each other, and each gave the other free rein to instruct the other's players.

The rest of the coaches used to tease Van Der Heyden about his reluctance to work on pass protections. He was a run-first coach just like Ford, and preferred to have his players fire off the ball and hit somebody in the mouth on every play.

Offensive coordinator Nelson Stokley said convincing Van Der Heyden that the passing game was important proved difficult.

"He liked to run the ball all the time and let the guys hit somebody and get after somebody," Stokley said. "He wasn't really thrilled with the passing game. But we kind of convinced him we had to do that [pass] in order to be a good football team."

KING AND REEDY: FORD'S CONFIDANTS

Buddy King was one of Ford's most trusted assistants because he had been on the staff since 1975, longer than anybody else working for Ford. King was a strong tactician who watched a ton of film and recruited excellently.

Running backs coach Chuck Reedy said that shortly after Bill Atchley replaced R.C. Edwards as university president in 1979, Ford brought him into the office Reedy shared with King. Ford introduced the president as "Dr. Atchley."

"Hey Doc, how are you doing?" Reedy remembered King saying. "Where are you from, Doc?"

Ford realized King had no idea who Atchley was and quickly explained that Atchley was the school's new president. King's face turned bright red as he realized his mistake.

Farr said King always had a wad of chewing tobacco in his mouth during practice. The guards and centers secretly enjoyed seeing King get angry.

"He'd be jawing at [the tackles], and pretty soon spit would start going everywhere and he'd start slurring with his mouth full," Farr said. "You couldn't help but laugh under your breath when you saw him chewing out the tackles. But he wasn't as intense as Coach Van Der Heyden. He was a little more laid back."

Chuck Reedy had wanted to coach in college so badly at age 29 that he sent letters to just about every college coach in the South, 100 in all.

He was hired at Kentucky, went to Clemson to coach running backs under Charley Pell and became a full-time college coach after Ford replaced Pell in 1979. Reedy wasn't as fiery as the coaches on the offensive line.

"He was easy to talk to," said tailback Chuck McSwain. "He expected the best out of you. He wanted the best out of practice, and he was a hard worker."

Reedy had a career plan all mapped out. He wanted to be a college coach by age 30, a coordinator by 35, and a head coach by 40. He missed the final goal by just three years when he became head coach at Baylor.

Like King, Reedy had coached with Ford under Pell. Though Reedy said Ford didn't play favorites among his assistant coaches, Reedy was one of Ford's closest confidants. Ford could count on Reedy to be honest with him when he was making a blunder.

One day before Clemson played Maryland, Ford came into a coaches' meeting upset because he thought Maryland was "imitating" Clemson.

"Everybody is looking around asking, 'What's he talking about?'" Reedy said. "And then we're like, he means 'intimidate.'"

Nobody wanted to correct Ford's English, but Reedy didn't want him going into his news conference later that day and confusing everybody with "imitate" when he meant "intimidate." Reedy called Ford aside and explained the difference.

Reedy said he had "pretty much been told" he would take over Clemson's head coaching job when Ford was finished there. The uneasy circumstances surrounding Ford's departure in 1989 caused Clemson to hire Ken Hatfield from Arkansas instead, but Reedy expected to be a candidate.

After Ford's buyout terms were finalized, he called Reedy at 1:00 a.m. to tell him he needed to start making phone calls in an effort to get the job. Reedy thanked Ford and told him how sorry he was that Ford was finished at Clemson.

Ford told him he was worried about the staff, not about himself.

"I picked up the paper the next day and saw he got a million-dollar payoff," Reedy said, laughing. "Now I know why he wasn't worried about himself."

DORM LIFE WAS HOLLAND'S OPUS

Lawson Holland received a call late one night from one of the women's dormitories on campus. He was asked to hustle over there and escort some football players—whom he won't name—back to the athletes' dorm at Mauldin Hall, where they belonged.

The NCAA now forbids athletes' dorms because it doesn't want athletes segregated from the general student population. In 1981, most of Clemson's players stayed in Mauldin Hall, and wide receivers coach Holland roomed there to keep an eye on them.

A Clemson alumnus, Holland married his wife, Cathy, a former Clemson cheerleader, in May of 1981. She was a schoolteacher who always had plenty of help from the players when it came time to unload the groceries from her car.

"It's probably the best financially we ever were in our lives," Holland said. "We had free rent. We had no phone bill, ate at the cafeteria."

Holland also had a difficult balancing act as a young member of the coaching staff at age 29. He wanted players to trust him because they were constantly under his supervision, but he couldn't be their buddy because he was one of their coaches. His ultimate loyalty was to Danny Ford and the football staff, but the coaches didn't want to know every little problem from the dorm.

"But if a guy got in serious trouble, it was my responsibility to look out for everybody else on the team as well because we had 99 percent of our guys doing right," Holland said.

What amazes Holland is how the players stuck together and the camaraderie that existed in that dorm. The players on the 1981 hung out with one another and seemed to enjoy one another's company.

They also policed one another. Holland vividly remembers senior linebacker Jeff Davis pinning massive freshman William Perry up against the door of the elevator one day. Davis told Perry he needed to get in the weight room and work hard because the team needed him to be a good player.

"We had such strong leadership on those teams," Holland said, "and Jeff was certainly one of the best leaders we had."

That made Holland's job easier.

TWICE A CHAMPION

Everyone in the locker room was "raising Cain" after the Orange Bowl victory, according to wide receivers coach Lawson Holland, so he retreated to the coaches' locker room for some peace.

He sat there and smoked four or five cigarettes with defensive coordinator Tom Harper, absorbing the magnitude of their achievement.

"What do you think?" Holland said Harper asked him.

"I don't know," Holland replied. "I don't know what to think."

Fifteen years later, Holland won another national championship on Steve Spurrier's staff at Florida. Holland said the parallels between the two championship teams were amazing. Both schools were winning their first national titles, and Holland believes both staffs benefited from following the late Charley Pell at their schools.

Holland credits Pell for building Clemson into a winning program and reinvigorating the IPTAY boosters with his magnetic personality. After leaving Clemson for Florida (and telling recruits that a national title couldn't be won at Clemson), Pell energized the Florida fan base. Holland has fond memories of speaking at a women's Gator fan club outing that he said Pell initiated.

"I feel like I've reaped rewards of Charley Pell twice," Holland said.

Holland has difficulty comparing the two national championship teams, though, because they were so different. He was a young coach who had been married less than a year when he sat in the coaches' locker room smoking with Harper and marveling that Clemson would be No. 1 when the final poll was announced. Holland said the incredible start spoiled him and his wife, Cathy, because they ultimately would learn in 28 years of coaching that the profession isn't nearly as easy as it seemed that first year.

Holland was more entrenched in the coaching profession 15 years later when he won with Florida. He said he appreciated the second championship more because he had a better understanding of the work and good fortune it takes to win a title.

"I've worked with and been friends with a lot of coaches that have gone through long careers, and their teams have never even competed for a conference championship," Holland said. "I think we were so fortunate to be a part of those teams."

Because it was more recent, Holland obviously has more vivid memories of the championship at Florida. The title at Clemson was special, though, because he is an alumnus.

"Certainly Clemson will win another one at some point in time," Holland said. "Florida will win another one at some point in time. But that's just so special to look back and say I was with a staff and a team that it's only been done one time in this history of those two schools. Will it happen again? Yeah, it will. But gosh, it's just amazing—of all the years that you're able to participate and be a part of it, that twice it's happened."

3

THE STARS:
Davis, Tuttle, Fridge, and More

" Jeff had this unusual work ethic, especially in the weight room. I would kind of follow his lead, and as he rallied the defensive team together, I took the initiative offensively. I really believe that we grew not just physically, being stronger and faster and running better routes. We kind of grew as a team. "

—Wide receiver Perry Tuttle

The most famous play in the Orange Bowl was the 13-yard touchdown pass from Homer Jordan to Perry Tuttle that immortalized Tuttle on the cover of *Sports Illustrated*.

Jordan and Tuttle practiced the play—a fade route—over and over again during practice. In the huddle, Jordan had a feeling they might use it. He told Tuttle to watch him. When he surveyed the defense after breaking the huddle, Jordan nodded to Tuttle that the fade was coming.

Split out to Jordan's left, Tuttle drew man-to-man coverage. Jordan threw a perfect pass, and Nebraska cornerback Allen Lyday never had a chance.

"I just laid it up, and he went and got it," Jordan said.

Tuttle's teammates said it's fitting that he received the national attention from the *Sports Illustrated* cover. Tuttle might be the most effervescent player from that team. Jordan says that, if you ever want to get to know a lot of people, you should hang out with Tuttle, because he knows everybody.

Nobody except for Tuttle's fourth-grade football coach, Pete Chitty, would have imagined it would turn out that way. Tuttle had failed third grade and thought himself stupid because of it. One day on the way home from practice, Tuttle was gazing silently out the window of Chitty's sky blue Ford Fairlane when it stopped in front of Hedrick's Feed Store in Midway, North Carolina.

"Perry, I believe that one day you're going to play in the NFL," Chitty told him.

Chitty's words breathed life into the once-shy boy. With an old football Chitty gave him, Tuttle played in his backyard, imagining he was playing for the Dallas Cowboys in sold-out Texas Stadium. He would throw the ball high into the sky, then run underneath and catch it, dreaming he was Bob Hayes, the speedy Cowboys receiver famous for his deep routes.

When he got to Clemson, he always believed he would be the player who caught the winning touchdown pass. Wearing Hayes' No. 22, he often infuriated teammate Jeff Stockstill in practice because he would come up gimpy with a sore hamstring or knee.

In front of a big crowd, it was a different story. Tuttle always was ready to seize the moment, and he did so on the game's biggest stage in the Orange Bowl.

"I was a gameday player," Tuttle said. "I practiced at it, but mostly I had gameday speed, and I was the kind of player that if I knew I could get my name in the paper, the better I played. And especially if a reporter interviewed me on a Wednesday or Thursday and I could read the story on a Saturday morning at the hotel, I was pumped up. That's the way I played."

Clemson wide receivers coach Lawson Holland said Tuttle had a rare, God-given gift of speed that set him apart from other players on the team. Tuttle said he wasn't much of a blocker, but Holland gives him credit for being better than he thinks.

In 1980 against North Carolina, Clemson ran a play called "19 crack" that called for a wide receiver to lead the option. Tuttle's job was to crack back and block the first defender standing up to the inside. That player happened to be Lawrence Taylor, who put Tuttle flat on his back.

Holland remembers their conversation when Tuttle came off the field afterward.

"Coach, I've always done anything you've asked," Holland said Tuttle told him. "But I'm not doing that again."

Holland said he didn't blame Tuttle for that, but also said Tuttle seldom backed down from anybody.

"Perry became a really good blocker because he wanted to," Holland said. "He wasn't the most ferocious guy, but boy, he would compete."

COVER BOY

The cover of the January 11, 1982, *Sports Illustrated* was the only one ever to feature an athlete performing for Clemson.

More than 20 years later, Tuttle is still signing copies of that magazine. He often signs four or five a month, and rarely goes a month without signing one.

"I keep thinking, 'Where are they coming from?'" Tuttle said. "I know they did a second run on them, and I'm just amazed."

Homer Jordan wasn't surprised Tuttle was the player who ended up on the magazine cover.

"He was that type of person, he knew the right people, was in the right place," Jordan said. "Things just happened for him. That's the way he is today."

Watching a videotape of the Orange Bowl victory one day with his former teammates, Tuttle realized that he almost never got to make his famous play. He shouted out to fullback Jeff McCall.

"If you didn't stumble, you would have scored," Tuttle said.

Three plays before Jordan passed to Tuttle, McCall busted through the line on first-and-10 from the 16. McCall broke into open field and saw the goal line, only to have a Nebraska defender dive and hit his heel, tripping him up just in time to prolong the drive.

McCall thought he was about to score anyway. He was one of the team's primary options in short yardage and goal line, and Nebraska certainly hadn't stopped him on the previous play. Running backs coach Chuck Reedy was congratulating him on a great run, and McCall was sure the staff would call another play for him.

Instead, they gave the ball to Chuck McSwain twice, and McSwain lost 10 yards on the second carry to set up third-and-goal from the 13— and the famous pass from Jordan to Tuttle.

The day after the Orange Bowl, Clemson's staff met Nebraska's at the postgame bowl banquet. Offensive coordinator Nelson Stokley spoke with a member of the Nebraska staff who had wanted to play zone on that play instead of man to man.

If he had gotten his way, Tuttle's life probably would have been much different. But others on the Nebraska staff decided to play man to man, and that played right into Clemson's hands.

"That's what you want," Stokley said, "your best receiver man to man on that cornerback."

DORMMATES

The trash talking that went back and forth between offense and defense in 1981 survives to this day. By telephone from his office at Clemson, where he serves as assistant athletics director for major gifts, linebacker Jeff Davis had a message for Tuttle.

"On several occasions, they will say it was the offense that won the national championship," Davis said, "and I want to make sure you put in this book that defense really does win championships, and any offense that couldn't score more than eight points a game—I wouldn't consider them an offense."

The players on defense in 1981 were so cocky that many players on offense wanted nothing to do with their counterparts. A notable exception to this division was the relationship of Tuttle and Davis, the vocal senior leaders on offense and defense, respectively, who hit it off quickly as roommates.

Davis and Tuttle quickly became close friends. Davis grew up without a father, and Tuttle's father was somewhat absent from his life, so they had something in common. Davis had a good singing voice and would sing silly songs and speak platitudes about life that he learned from his high school coach, Jonathan McKee.

"Kill a gnat with a sledgehammer," was one, and it meant that a player should always give a first-rate effort and leave nothing to chance.

"It wasn't enough for us to tackle a guy," Davis said. "When we tackled him, we wanted to make sure his head hit the ground."

During spring practice, Davis and Tuttle didn't always get along because that's when the first-team offense and defense scrimmaged each other the most.

"I'm going to take up for the offense, and he's going to do his deal for the defense," Tuttle said. "But during the season, we really enjoyed each other."

They became like brothers. They talked about their high school days at first ("That's what freshmen would do. You can always tell who the freshmen are," said Tuttle). As time went on, Davis began talking about his future in his football. Tuttle loved hearing Davis' plans. Tuttle was laid back and relaxed, and watching the extremely motivated Davis' devotion inspired him.

Davis would go from class to class, work out and come back to the room buff and intense about winning, and Tuttle wanted to match him. At night, especially during their senior season, they would lie in bed and talk about their dreams for their team, about winning a national championship. They would turn out the lights, and Tuttle would throw the ball toward the ceiling in the dark, one time, 50 times, 100 times, feeling it instead of seeing it, developing muscle memory that would serve him well on the field.

Their heartfelt conversations about winning a national title proved prophetic, in part perhaps because they were building a winning spirit as they talked.

"We kind of just grew up together in this dormitory, fantasizing about being something special, and football gave us the stage to shine," Tuttle said. "The friendship we had was because of football."

FOLLOWING THE LEADER

During spring practice, when the first-team offense and defense scrimmaged often, there was one blocking call that center Tony Berryhill despised.

It was called a "slant pick," and it made the center and backside guard responsible for the nose guard and the backside linebacker. Often, it meant that Berryhill would have to block Jeff Davis, a task he dreaded.

"If I hit him high, he was going to kill me with his forearms, so I had to hit him low," Berryhill said. "Of course, going out there and cutting him on his thigh was like running into a pine tree. The other linebackers, you could cut them, and they would go to the ground pretty quick. But Jeff, he was tough."

Davis was the unquestioned leader of the team. Other players became better pros, but Davis made an astounding 175 tackles in 1981 and supplied motivation the likes of which Clemson athletics has probably never seen. In 1995, he was enshrined in the Ring of Honor, the highest honor Clemson athletics can bestow.

"He was one of the best linebackers I've ever seen," said quarterback Homer Jordan. "I think he bench pressed 525 or something like that, and squatted 1,000 pounds, it seemed like. I'm glad he was on our team."

Fullback Jeff McCall occasionally was called upon to block Davis and was one of the few players to succeed at it. McCall said Davis used to accuse him of being sneaky with his blocks.

Whatever the case, running backs coach Chuck Reedy must have noticed, because one day he taunted Davis in the cafeteria.

"Yeah, yeah, yeah, yeah," McCall recalled Reedy saying. "I've got somebody to block you now."

Davis must have been looking for McCall in the next practice. McCall was cutting back and preparing to block Davis, who had both arms cocked. There was a terrible collision.

McCall, one of the ACC's biggest, toughest blocking backs, went down on two knees.

He wasn't so woozy that he couldn't hear Davis taunting.

"Yeah, yeah, yeah, yeah," McCall said Davis told him. "I've got something for you."

One day after practice, defensive backs coach Curley Hallman had determined that one of his players would be punished for having a poor attitude. Hallman planned to make the player run extra sprints, but a bunch of seniors, led by Davis, stopped him.

"Let us handle it," Hallman said Davis told him.

They didn't make the player run. They simply told him that if he didn't stop pouting, then he didn't have to worry about ever playing anymore, because they wouldn't have him on their team. Hallman didn't have any more problems with that player.

"You can imagine a lot of the stuff that took place when the coaches weren't around," Hallman said. "The players would handle stuff, and we'd never hear about it. That's what great leadership is all about, when players can take care of certain situations without the coaches getting involved."

In such situations Davis was always the leader.

FINDING HIS FATHER

Davis remembers being in elementary school when his friends were talking about their fathers one day.

They asked him about his father. He said he didn't have one. Afterward, one of his friends discreetly took him aside. The friend explained that he had to have a father. If he didn't, he wouldn't exist.

"I had never thought about it like that," Davis said. "The only thing I knew was he was absent."

Davis went home that day and asked his mother, Charlene Davis, about his father. He could tell by the look on her face that he'd asked the wrong question, and she didn't give him any kind of explanation.

So he counted on other men in his life to give him direction. The most influential among them was Jonathan McKee, who coached Davis at Dudley High in Greensboro, North Carolina.

They remain close today. McKee believed success in football would correlate with success in life, and he instilled that philosophy in Davis.

"His whole philosophy was that winning wasn't limited to an arena," Davis said. "It was a way of life. Winners don't always win, but they don't ever quit. They don't ever quit. He would instill that in me."

When he was inducted into the South Carolina Athletic Hall of Fame, Davis paid tribute to McKee by singing Clemson's alma mater. McKee always required that, win or lose, his players would sing their alma mater before and after a game.

Following the hall of fame banquet, a South Carolina Gamecocks fan approached Davis. The fan said it pained him to admit this, because he was a Gamecock, but he had never seen a player honor his institution in such a touching way.

"He helped me think about what my high school coach taught me [about the alma mater]," Davis said. "What he taught me was still alive then, and it's still well respected today—and it's a part of who I am."

McKee also played a role in one of the most incredible experiences of Davis' adult life. Davis was 33 when his daughter, Jenne, began asking about his father. She had met her maternal grandparents and Charlene Davis, and she wanted to know if her father had a father.

Davis approached his mother again. He said he couldn't tell his daughter that he didn't know who his father was. So his mother revealed his father's name. Apparently, Tony Couch didn't even know Jeff Davis existed, but Davis didn't make any attempt to contact him.

About a month later, Davis was talking with McKee, who often had asked Davis what he knew about his father. This time, Davis had an answer for him.

McKee said he knew Tony Couch. McKee had never made the connection before, but said their mannerisms were remarkably similar. The coach set up a meeting. Davis estimates that he spoke with his father for an hour or two before introducing his wife and children, because he was so excited to meet his father.

"It was so overwhelming, and it was such a part of my life that I didn't know much about," Davis said. "To see this person you look like, to see this person that is your father, it's really like you're a little kid. I was really kind of blown away by that, because I was a father myself."

Davis and Couch have remained in touch, and Couch's first football experience with Davis was his induction into Clemson's Ring of Honor at Memorial Stadium in 1995. Couch attended with Charlene Davis, whom he hadn't seen in more than 30 years, and handled the whole situation with class.

"For him to be able to experience one of the highest honors for me at Clemson was really fulfilling," Davis said. "While he didn't see the journey, he got to see one of the greatest ways it could be culminated. It's been quite an experience."

PIZZA WITH THE FRIDGE

In 1980, William Perry made a visit to Clemson as a high school senior. Perry Tuttle and Jeff Davis were his player hosts. They took Perry downtown for pizza, and Perry spoke first when the waitress arrived at the table. He ordered two large pizzas.

"I thought he was pretty bold to order for all of us," Tuttle said.

Then Perry looked at Tuttle and Davis and asked what they were ordering. Their jaws dropped, and they were even more incredulous as they watched the giant devour both his pizzas. He would take two slices of pizza and fold them together like a sandwich. When he ate, it appeared as though he inhaled without even chewing.

"I just stared at him the whole time," Tuttle said, "and just laughed, and said, 'Who is this guy?'"

Defensive end Steve Berlin was in the same high school class as Perry and visited campus one day when Perry was there. Berlin was at Memorial Stadium with assistant coach Larry Van Der Heyden when he saw Perry. Berlin was a big high school senior at that time, about 6 feet, 5 inches tall and 240 pounds, but he couldn't believe the size of Perry.

Berlin saw Perry and figured he was one of the Tigers' alumni playing in the NFL and visiting campus. He gawked at Perry's broad shoulders and asked who he was. He was stunned when he was told Perry was a high school senior committed to Clemson.

"I said, 'Boy, am I in trouble,'" Berlin said.

Tight end Bubba Diggs was redshirting in 1980 because of a bone chip in his elbow and attended many of Perry's high school games because he wasn't traveling with the Clemson team. Perry was from Aiken, South Carolina, and Diggs was from Augusta, Georgia, so Diggs knew his way around that area.

Diggs couldn't believe what he was seeing as Perry physically overpowered high school players. He also was shocked to see Perry play basketball at nearly 300 pounds. Diggs thought Perry would just park himself on the block and crash the boards. Instead, Perry got the ball on a fast break, drove to the basket, and dunked.

Later, Diggs was getting ready to play pickup basketball at Fike Fieldhouse when Jeff Davis and some other teammates were picking teams. Nobody would pick Perry because they figured he wouldn't be any good at his size, but Diggs was pleading with somebody to ask him to be on their team. When Perry got a chance to play, he dominated in the post.

"He showed them he could play the game and bump and grind down low anyway," Diggs said, laughing.

The first time Berlin saw Perry play basketball, there were about 40 players gathered at a court outside Schilleter Dining Hall. They were playing rough-and-tumble pickup ball in an atmosphere similar to an inner-city playground—where only the strongest survive and are allowed to remain on the court.

Perry grabbed the ball and threw down one of the most vicious dunks Berlin has ever seen. The pole holding the backboard moved so violently under the force of Perry's weight that Berlin was afraid the whole apparatus might crash to the ground.

"Perry kind of had a chip on his shoulder," Berlin said. "He wanted to prove himself to these guys, and it didn't take very long."

Clemson's coaches encouraged Perry to keep his weight down any way he could. Basketball was good for burning calories, as was swimming.

Tailback Chuck McSwain remembers marveling at Perry at the pool.

"You'd see 300 pounds hit that board, and it would about bend to the water," McSwain said. "It was amazing."

Berlin was among the first players on Clemson's campus to see Perry swim. They worked out together during summer school following their freshman year. Berlin was fascinated with Perry and wanted to learn what made him tick.

Together they would run the dikes surrounding Lake Hartwell near Jervey Athletic Center. One day, after they ran, Perry suggested they swim. Berlin was surprised, but agreed to swim with Perry at the Fike Recreation Center.

When they arrived at the pool, Perry asked Berlin whether he should do a backflip or just dive into the pool. Berlin was flabbergasted. He imagined that if Perry jumped in, all the water would spill over the sides of the pool.

Perry goaded Berlin into betting him that he couldn't do a back flip into the pool. Then Perry walked to the end of the board, and bent it about to the water when he jumped on it. The board flipped Perry back into the air, and he performed a perfect back flip. He entered the water without a splash, stunning Berlin and winning the wager.

"I about had heart failure when I saw that," Berlin said. "I could not believe this guy was so graceful. He jumped out of the water, laughing. He had a big smile on his face."

Then Perry climbed to the top of the high diving board and repeated the maneuver. Berlin began to realize just how special Perry was—something his teammates would learn later.

Keeping in shape was a constant struggle for Perry, though. One of the most difficult times for Perry was the preseason, when the coaching staff worked the players back into shape. One of the post-summer workouts consisted of running up and down the dikes of Lake Hartwell near campus.

The linemen had a set amount of time in which to complete their run. Perry couldn't make his time, but managed to drag his tremendous bulk up and down the dikes.

"I remember him barely being able to get up and down that dike on a hot day," said wide receiver Jerry Gaillard.

'HE WAS HUGE'

Perry became so big and was so difficult to block that at times during spring practice, Ford would make him stand on the sideline.

Ford would taunt the offensive linemen, telling them that he wouldn't let Perry practice if they couldn't block him.

Berryhill was the player whose misfortune it was to line up across from William Perry in practice.

Van Der Heyden had the line do a drill during which he would stand behind the defensive linemen. He would give the offensive linemen instructions for their blocks by pointing.

If Van Der Heyden pointed at himself, it meant the offensive linemen were to drive their man straight off the ball. This was akin to suicide for whomever was lined up across from Perry.

Danny Ford coached the time-honored football truism that the player lowest to the ground gets the advantage in any blocking situation. Berryhill listened and obeyed, to the point where he was only 12 inches off the ground after snapping the ball when it came time to drive Perry off the ball.

"And if I stood up, he was going to take my head off," Berryhill said. "Needless to say, I never moved him. He was huge."

Dan Benish is pretty sure the following story about William Perry was from Perry's sophomore season, but it's too good not to share.

Perry reported to camp overweight, and the coaches were not happy. They told Perry he needed to eat bananas, perhaps figuring he would lose weight if they loaded him up with simple sugars he could burn off quickly rather than fats and complex carbohydrates.

Apparently Perry thought the coaches were trying to tell him that bananas were all he was allowed to eat. One day during two-a-days, he made a quick exit after the morning practice. He didn't bother to shower, threw on shorts and a T-shirt and hopped on the bus to go to the dining hall for lunch.

Benish was one of the first players to arrive at the dining hall after Perry, and he couldn't believe his eyes. Perry's tray was piled high with bananas.

"You couldn't get any more banana peels on that tray," Benish said. "He took every banana that was on the fruit tray and ate every single one of them."

Benish said Perry was known for being gentle off the field despite his intimidating girth.

Fullback Jeff McCall remembers that Perry wasn't always so gentle on the field. One day during a practice at the stadium, the offense called a counter play. The plan was to let Perry break through the line, then have McCall pull back and block Perry. It worked perfectly.

Just when Perry thought he was about to make the tackle, McCall pulled back and cut him with a low block, bringing him to the ground.

Perry barked at McCall, claiming McCall had clipped him. McCall denied it. Next thing he knew, Perry had removed his helmet and was charging after him. McCall didn't stick around to find out what Perry planned to do to him. He removed his helmet and fled.

"I'm not fighting that big guy," McCall said. "Uh-uh."

JORDAN'S WILD DAY

Homer Jordan's day at the Orange Bowl began with a jittery awakening and ended with a woozy collapse.

Jordan couldn't sleep as he anticipated the biggest game of his life. He woke up Perry Tuttle 15 hours before the game and shared some nervous words.

By halftime, the long day and the heat had taken their toll. Jordan felt queasy in the locker room. He hung on long enough to make the run that just about clinched the victory on a sprintout in the fourth quarter.

After running 21 yards for a first down, Jordan lay on the ground for a long time, until a teammate came to help him up.

"I was so tired," he said.

Jordan celebrated on the field with Tuttle, then fainted on the way to the locker room.

"They gave me an IV and all that stuff and said I'd better take it easy," Jordan said.

Dr. Byron Harder remembers players calling for him and the other team physician, Dr. Jud Hair, after Jordan collapsed. They were over Jordan in an instant, and Harder barely felt a pulse.

Homer Jordan's irrepressible enthusiasm made it easy for him to succeed as Clemson's first black starting quarterback.

Harder took Jordan's blood pressure and got a dangerously low reading of about 60 on the upper reading, and couldn't get a lower reading.

Because the blood pressure was so low, the doctors had difficulty finding a vein in each arm for the IVs to restore Jordan's body fluids.

"We thought he was pretty bad off," Harder said. "He came around really quick. It was a big relief to us."

BOOGIE MAN

They called senior defensive tackle Jeff Bryant "Boogie Man," and from across the line of scrimmage, he must have looked like a monster.

He was 6 feet, 5 inches tall and 257 pounds, with long arms that prevented opposing offensive linemen from getting into his body and knocking him off stride as he came around the end. His wrestling success—Bryant was 18-0 with 14 pins in his senior year at Gordon High in Atlanta—helped him learn how to use his long arms and legs as leverage in football. He also had the admiration of his younger teammates because of his laid-back, fun-loving personality, his deep, booming voice, and the rap music he enjoyed.

"He was the man," said fellow defensive tackle Steve Berlin, a freshman in 1981. "He was just 6-6, 6-7, bowlegged, and I just thought he was the coolest guy I ever met."

Bryant entered the 1981 season as a solid but unspectacular player despite his great physical talent. He made 52 tackles to lead the Clemson defensive linemen, but just seven behind the line of scrimmage in 1980.

First-year defensive coordinator Tom Harper changed all that in 1981. He devised a scheme to get more one-on-one opportunities for Bryant. He didn't want Bryant reading and reacting to the offense. He asked Bryant to use his superior talent to get into the backfield and disrupt plays as quickly as possible.

"He played to our strengths," said fellow defensive tackle Dan Benish. "Jeff Bryant will tell you that Tom Harper really helped his career out. He turned him loose and just had him go for the passer."

Thus liberated, Bryant had a monster season in 1981. He made 92 tackles—a huge number for a defensive lineman—with 19 behind the line of scrimmage, including eight sacks.

His best game probably was the defensive struggle against North Carolina, when he made 11 tackles and two sacks and recovered a fumbled lateral pass in the fourth quarter to clinch a 10-8 victory for the Tigers.

Bryant was named second-team All-America by *Football News*, and followed through on the promise Harper saw in him in the NFL draft the following April. Drafted with the sixth pick of the first round by Seattle, he enjoyed a long, productive 12-year career in the NFL.

"He had really long legs, and he was fast," Benish said. "He came out of his stance and was able to swing his arm up and get his arm on the guy's shoulder pads, and they didn't have a chance. He just played that right end spot perfectly, I thought. He didn't worry about the run. He just got penetration upfield and screwed everything up."

BETTER THAN BRETT?

Curley Hallman, who coached linebackers and defensive backs at Clemson and went on to become head coach at Southern Mississippi, occasionally is asked if Brett Favre was the best college player he ever coached.

"I say no," Hallman said. "I always thought he could be a great player someday, but in college, he was not a great player—he was going to be if he kept working. It's obvious now that was true."

Hallman said Terry Kinard, Clemson's free safety, might be the best college player he ever coached. Kinard was named to *Sports Illustrated*'s All-Century team in 1999 as one of college football's best safeties ever.

"I think a truly great player makes all those other people around him better players," Hallman said. "They will play better than they are supposed to play. Terry could do that. He could dominate a ballgame at free safety on defense."

Kinard could have—and perhaps should have—attended rival South Carolina. He played for the Sumter High Gamecocks and grew up watching Gamecock football. He didn't have cable TV or an outdoor antenna at his house, so he couldn't get Clemson games on television. He watched South Carolina on TV and dreamed of playing football there.

That changed when he was being recruited.

"I had a bad experience when I went to the University of South Carolina on my recruiting trip," Kinard said. "I didn't like the guys at all. They were cocky, a bunch of arrogant guys, and it wasn't the situation I wanted to be in."

Clemson was completely different. "It felt like home," Kinard said, "and the players seemed like decent guys." Defensive ends coach Willie Anderson recruited Kinard and did a marvelous job.

It helped that Anderson was from Mayesville, 10 miles away from where Kinard grew up. Anderson made a great impression on Kinard's mother, and Kinard eagerly decided to attend Clemson.

The amazing thing about Kinard is that he apparently had no idea just how talented he was when he entered Clemson. Recruiting coverage in the media was in its infant stages, so prospects usually entered school without the big egos that accompany many freshmen now on college campuses.

Kinard liked the school and saw that Clemson had two senior free safeties about to complete their eligibility, so he thought he might have a chance to help the Tigers immediately.

"I just wanted to have the opportunity to continue to play," Kinard said. "You don't even think about how great the situation was. For me, in my heart, all I knew was it would be a shame to be like a lot of those kids that didn't get an opportunity to play anymore when you love a sport the way I loved it. To get the opportunity to play, that was it for me."

Kinard went on to an incomparable career at Clemson. He intercepted 17 passes, setting a school record that still stands, and remains Clemson's only two-time, first-team Associated Press All-American. He later won Super Bowl XXI with the New York Giants. In recent years, he received Clemson's top athletics honor as an inductee in the school's Ring of Honor and became the school's second member (along with Banks McFadden) of the College Football Hall of Fame.

4

THE PLAYERS:
From Jughead to George Patton

" When you think about it, there were no superstars. There were no Herschel Walkers or Matt Leinarts. There were just 60 guys that just got along great, and I can't recall ever having any problems amongst anybody on the team. "

—Holder Anthony Parete

Offensive linemen almost universally are pranksters, and Clemson's were no different.

They had a word for what happened to freshmen during the preseason, when they were so overwhelmed and exhausted that they looked like they wanted to quit the team and go home. The linemen called that particular brand of insanity, "It-ing."

Before practice every day, the linemen would go upstairs to a meeting room to watch film. They would turn off the lights and begin to make fun of one another during what they called "It" sessions—playfully trying to drive one another nuts.

They all had nicknames that were used during these sessions. Guard James Farr was "Granitehead." Tackle Brad Fisher was "Airplane." Center Tony Berryhill was "Jughead," because he had the smallest head on the team.

One favored mode of humor was to insult teammates' mothers. Berryhill was one of the instigators, and he regularly made fun of the women who raised his teammates.

He also seemed to have a foolproof way to insulate himself from retaliatory ribbing. He told his mother that she should never give her name to anybody who called the house asking for her name.

In the days before the Internet and databases storing folks' personal information, this seemed to be enough to guard his mother's identify. Then one day Brian Butcher had a question for Berryhill as they sat in the meeting room with the lights off for an "It" session.

"How's Celia doing?" Butcher asked.

Berryhill was stunned. His mother had followed his advice and concealed her identity. Berryhill never imagined that his grandmother would trip him up.

"[Butcher] had called in and talked to my grandmother," Berryhill said. "Not only did he get my mother's name, he got my grandmother's name."

The jokes were twice as frequent because of it.

Knowing all those mothers' names also served a purpose on the field. The linemen had to change their blocking calls often during the game because opponents quickly would figure out what the initial calls meant. Players would create new calls throughout the game for each blocking scheme and also would create "dummy" calls that meant absolutely nothing and served merely to distract the defense.

Many times they used their mothers' names to call out real and fake blocking schemes. Perhaps the favorite name of all was "Mazell"— guard James Farr's mother's name. Farr said he never told his teammates her name, but believes they got it from his sister.

"They enjoyed that name," Farr said. "They had fun with that. It didn't seem to be the everyday name of Debbie or Patty, just a common name."

Other jokes were of the common college prank variety, and teammates weren't always the targets. Players would dump a trash can full of water off the third floor on the pizza man or throw water balloons at students.

They would put shaving cream on teammates' phones and then call them. They would slide baby powder under a teammate's door, then turn on a hair dryer and blow it throughout the room.

The identities of some pranksters remained concealed for decades. Berryhill was coming out of his dorm once and going to his car when he was hit twice in the head with rocks. A bunch of guys who had been loitering scattered when Berryhill turned around. The only one who didn't run was Reid Ingle, so Berryhill figured he had nothing to do with it.

During a reunion at Clemson's spring game in 2004, Ingle confessed.

"He finally told me he was the one that did it," Berryhill said.

FARM BOY

James Farr was a throwback to a time when Clemson was a school with deep agricultural roots.

Students who grew up on farms had been attending Clemson, a land grant institution, for generations. Farr was raised on a dairy farm. In the summer, he got up at 2:30 or three o'clock in the morning to help his father, Bob Farr, feed and milk the cows.

Farr said his upbringing was the reason for his success. He carried just 217 pounds on his 6-foot-4 frame as a sophomore starter, but thrived because of his toughness.

"Whatever you are brought up to do is what's instilled in you," Farr said. "Going through three-a-days, I didn't like it that much. But it didn't bother me because when I was on the farm a lot of days I didn't feel like working on the farm, but it's something you have to do. I was used to it."

Farr made up for his lack of size with quickness and agility. Clemson's play calls took advantage of those skills. Farr's favorite personal moment in 1981 came on a screen pass when he pulled out to block on the corner.

Playing in pain with his ribs taped up because of an injury suffered the week before, Farr delivered a crushing block.

"The guards at Clemson did a lot of pulling, and I loved that," he said. "I loved to pull and loved to trap and pull out on the linebackers and pull out on the defensive backs. That's just what we were drilled to do."

RECRUITING ODDITIES

A number of players on the national championship team had interesting stories about how they got to Clemson. Dan Benish, Jerry Gaillard, and Chuck McSwain had some of the best.

Benish, the starting left defensive tackle, came to the Tigers as an indirect result of Charlie Bauman's famous interception for Clemson in the 1978 Gator Bowl.

Ohio State coach Woody Hayes was fired after he slugged Bauman following his game-clinching interception. The following weekend, Benish, who is from Hubbard, Ohio, went to the airport to fly to Columbus for an official visit to Ohio State.

The weather in Ohio was miserable, and Benish's mother grumbled about the snow as she drove Benish and a friend, Duane Sell, to the airport. Sell was traveling to Clemson for an official visit. Ohio State was supposed to leave a plane ticket for Benish at the gate, but when he arrived, there was no ticket for him. Benish called an Ohio State assistant coach, who told him that Hayes had taken all his recruiting files with him, so the Buckeyes' staff was not expecting him.

"I thought, well, these guys don't want me that bad," Benish said. "And I had dreamed my whole life about going to Ohio State."

Sell encouraged Benish to accompany him to Clemson, which had expressed interest in Benish. Within a half-hour of Benish contacting the Clemson staff, Danny Ford had a ticket for him at the airport.

The trip went perfectly. It was sunny and about 70 degrees, and Benish was impressed with the friendliness of people in Clemson. He left Clemson knowing that was where he wanted to spend his college career.

"I went on two other recruiting trips after that," Benish said, "but nothing compared to Clemson."

Sell's story didn't end as happily. Clemson had just one scholarship left and offered it to Benish. Sell wound up at Bowling Green.

Gaillard believes he never would have made it to Clemson without the help of his uncle, Clarence Gaillard.

Gaillard was an "army brat." He attended 13 different schools in 12 years and played football at high schools in South America, Alabama, and Yuma, Arizona. He wasn't highly recruited because he didn't stay in one place long enough for anybody to keep track of him.

Auburn had demonstrated some interest in him, along with Alabama, Wake Forest, and a few other schools, but Gaillard wanted to go to Clemson to play wide receiver. He was born in Anderson, South Carolina, and his extended family, including his grandmother, Marie Gaillard, lived in and around Seneca, South Carolina.

Clarence Gaillard became his nephew's advocate with the Clemson coaching staff. He went to Jervey Athletic Center, where the coaches' offices were, and camped out there with videotapes of Jerry Gaillard in action.

Uncle Clarence bothered the coaches every day, until they finally agreed to screen his tapes. Apparently they liked what they saw, because Clemson sent assistant coach Tom Bass to Arizona for a visit, offered Gaillard a scholarship, and signed him.

Sadly, Clarence never got to see Jerry play at Clemson. He died of a heart attack in his mid-60s before Jerry's freshman season began.

McSwain chose Clemson even though its coach tried to convince him to go elsewhere.

Here's how that played out. The late coach Charley Pell was recruiting McSwain, who played high school football in Caroleen, North Carolina. McSwain said Pell told him he was leaving for Florida because Clemson could never win the national championship. Pell asked McSwain to come with him to Florida.

McSwain listened and weighed his options. He talked to others on the coaching staff and found out that many of the Clemson assistants were gong to stay there. When Danny Ford—who had been offensive coordinator—was promoted to head coach, McSwain was pleased.

Ford made a good impression on McSwain's family. McSwain said other coaches would visit McSwain in Caroleen and eat at restaurants. Ford came to McSwain's house and ate green beans and corn like everybody else.

"Danny would come in and he really didn't talk much about football," McSwain said. "He talked about family and meeting people and talked to my other sisters and kids. He was just a good, down-to-earth guy, and that's what helped him out more than anything. It got to the point where you wanted to play for him."

OH, BROTHER

Chuck and Rod McSwain were the 10th and 11th siblings in a family of 13 children raised by Custom (pronounced CUE-stom) and Dorothy McSwain in a three-bedroom house in Caroleen, North Carolina.

The McSwains made room for all their children by using roll-away beds, which they tucked away under the main beds in each bedroom. At night, they rolled the beds out—there were four in the room where Chuck and Rod slept—and put the children to bed side by side.

"I always tell the story that, when I was growing up, I never fell out of a bed," Chuck McSwain said. "... You could roll from one bed to another all the way across the room."

Chuck and Rod weren't unusual as a brother tandem on the same team at Clemson. Tiger fans recall William and Michael Dean Perry and twins Andy and Peter Ford among some of the more productive brotherhoods in school history along with the McSwains. Chuck was a junior tailback who split time with Cliff Austin. Rod was a sophomore and the top backup at cornerback.

Chuck chose Clemson because he was comfortable with the small-town atmosphere there and was charmed by a coach, Danny Ford, who chewed tobacco and wouldn't change his country image no matter who was around.

Rod chose Clemson because his brother was there, and though they had fought often growing up, they were inseparable. By their own choice, they were roommates at Clemson, and they treasure the time they spent together in college.

Even though Chuck had decided to attend Clemson, he visited Georgia Tech and Notre Dame mostly because he wanted to fly on an airplane, which he had never done before.

Because the McSwains had such a large family, they rarely traveled far. There wasn't a big enough vehicle to move them all. Clemson's Orange Bowl trip was the first time Chuck McSwain had ever been to the beach, even though he lived just five hours from the coastal cities of Myrtle Beach and Wilmington.

"When we would go out to eat, you'd get one order of fries or get one hamburger," Chuck McSwain said. "You didn't get both."

The boys didn't even understand how to order room service when they stayed in hotels on their official visits. They visited the University of Tennessee together and called down and ordered some food.

After some time passed, a member of the hotel staff rolled a cart into the room. There were plates on the cart with food on them, but the boys couldn't see it because there were metal covers over the plates to keep them warm.

About an hour passed, and Chuck called again to ask where their food was.

"We brought it up," Chuck was told.

"No, I don't see it," he replied.

He had no idea there was food on the cart.

The McSwains' finest game at Clemson came against South Carolina during that 1981 season. Chuck rushed for a season-high 151 yards on 25 carries and scored two touchdowns. Rod got Clemson's scoring started by blocking a punt that Johnny Rembert recovered in the end zone.

Three years later, the McSwains had a thrill that rivaled winning the national championship. Rod, a rookie with the New England Patriots, traveled to Dallas to meet Chuck and the Cowboys on Thanksgiving Day in front of a national television audience.

Their parents were in the stands, and Dorothy McSwain was holding a Patriots flag and a Cowboys flag, one for each son. Dallas won 20-17.

"We won the game," Chuck said, "but just the opportunity for two brothers to play opposite each other on the same day was something special."

Chuck was Clemson's first ACC rookie of the year in 1979. In 1981, he missed all but two weeks of preseason practice because of a deep thigh bruise and was bothered by the injury for the first three games. He still managed to rush for 692 yards and seven touchdowns on 144 carries.

Rod McSwain had excellent speed like his brother, but was lacking a bit in flexibility. He was 6 feet, 2 inches tall and 190 pounds—big for a cornerback—and rotated into games regularly. Defensive backs coach Curley Hallman said Rod's only physical shortcoming was his flexibility. Rod often complained of lower back pain, especially when he was tired.

"He might have been a little stiff in that lower back there; but boy, could he run," Hallman said.

FROM HOSPITAL TO GRIDIRON

Nobody considers himself more fortunate to have played a part in the national championship season than defensive end Ray Brown.

In 1980, Brown fell ill on Clemson's trip to Virginia to play the Cavaliers. He thought he had the flu, but the next thing he knew, he was headed to the intensive care unit at a local hospital.

Brown had spinal meningitis. He became virtually paralyzed on one side of his body. He dropped about 50 pounds in a month. He spent about 12 days in the hospital and months recovering. He believes his illness and the resulting concern of his teammates over his health were contributing factors that prevented the Tigers from finishing better than 6-5 in 1980.

It wasn't until the summer of 1981 that Brown even thought he might be able to play football again. He wasn't allowed to even practice until a neurologist okayed him.

"I probably wasn't recovered until the end of the national championship season," Brown said. "You just don't lose that and try to rebuild back your strength in that short a period."

Tight end Bubba Diggs was another player who was lucky to be alive, let alone playing football, in 1981.

Diggs had all sorts of injury problems. The summer before his freshman season, he broke his collarbone diving to make a catch while running pass routes with Steve Fuller, Jerry Butler, Dwight Clark, and others.

A chipped bone in his elbow forced him to redshirt in the 1980 season. Diggs' brush with death came when he was a freshman in 1979. One Sunday in early November, he decided to drive home to Augusta, Georgia, because there wasn't going to be a team meeting that evening. Diggs' roommate, Terry Kinard, was in the hospital recovering from shoulder surgery. Diggs was a bit homesick and just wanted to get away from campus for a day, so he borrowed Kinard's orange Datsun.

As Diggs tells it, two cars behind him were driving extremely fast, and he was concerned that they might rear-end him. Instead, one passed him on the left and another passed him in the median. Diggs said he was distracted and lost control of his car and ran off the road into a telephone pole and a tree.

He recovered in time to practice later that month and play in the regular-season finale against South Carolina. Two days later, Diggs was in the hospital, having emergency surgery to have a ruptured spleen removed. He had felt pain in his midsection earlier, but it was attributed to bruised ribs.

"I consider myself very, very fortunate," he said

Diggs considered giving up football after that. He lost 30 pounds and went to spring practice as a 200-pound tight end. Needless to say, his teammates were throwing him around like a rag doll.

But he is glad he didn't give up and is extremely proud of his status as a national champion. His father gave him an eight-millimeter camera to take video, and he still watches his home movies of media day at the Orange Bowl, the hotel in Miami, and other memorable things a few times a year.

He has a Clemson wall of fame in his house for important paraphernalia, and only allows mementos of Clemson and the pro teams he has represented displayed in his house. That's not difficult because his two daughters aren't huge sports fans, but it certainly shows the depth of his love and respect for Clemson.

"I think this particular team is a very, very special team," Diggs said. "Each and every team is special, but that year you can't take away from Clemson University."

COME BACK, MACK

Talking Kevin Mack out of quitting football became a routine during Mack's freshman season in 1980 at Clemson.

Mack, the fleet-footed fullback, often left the practice field with intentions of returning home to Kings Mountain, North Carolina, because he was homesick. The players would approach the coaches and explain that Mack was gone again, headed to the locker room.

"We'd have to take off and run up there and go get him," said tailback Chuck McSwain. "Then after a while the coaches would go get him. ... He quit several times his freshman year. We'd be in the locker room, and he'd just get homesick, and that happens a lot of places. He quit several times."

McSwain, who was from Caroleen, North Carolina, often did the honors because he had known Mack long before they got to Clemson. McSwain and Mack were track rivals in high school. McSwain would talk to Mack, telling him he would be going home on the upcoming weekend and would bring Mack home, too.

Mack stayed on the team and became the most successful back from the national championship team in the pros. He weighed just 197 pounds but ran as hard as a 250-pound fullback.

In 1985, Mack rushed for 1,104 yards for the Cleveland Browns.

Years later, fellow fullback Jeff McCall was playing for the Los Angeles Raiders and visited Mack, who was a member of the USFL's Los Angeles Express.

"Mack had gotten drafted pretty high, and I walked in to see Mack, and said, 'Mack, see, you almost quit your sophomore year. And look at you now.' He said, 'I know.'"

TAUNTS AND DRY HEAVES

Clemson cornerback Hollis Hall was ahead of his time.

Hall grew up practically in the shadow of Death Valley in Seneca and was a pioneer in the field of trash talking, which wasn't common on football fields until at least 10 years after Hall elevated it to an art form at Clemson.

When he made a big hit on a wide receiver or running back, Hall would taunt them.

"You don't want to come back here," teammate Anthony Rose remembers him saying. "It's going to be like that all day."

Then, as Hall walked back to the huddle, he would deliver the perfect parting shot.

"Oh, by the way," Rose remembers Hall saying, "it's the same way on the other side."

Rose gives most of the credit for Clemson's defensive success to the front seven and free safety Terry Kinard, who could run down just about any opponent in the open field and had incredible closing speed to break up and intercept passes. The senior starting cornerbacks—Rose and Hall—often are overlooked but played huge roles, too.

Hall, who went on to play two seasons in the USFL, had the quickness, technique, and savvy to blanket any receiver. He had confidence, too, which is an important trait for a defensive back often left alone in man-to-man situations. He wasn't afraid to let everybody on offense know that nobody was going to catch a big pass against him.

That attitude helped Rose, who was less athletic and sometimes needed a confidence boost.

"With him giving that type of verbiage on the other side, I couldn't let it be dead on this side," Rose said.

Rose came to Clemson as a walk-on, in part because his friend, Kinard, had been recruited there. Rose and Kinard grew up in Sumter together, and though they went to separate high schools, they worked on the same Fort Roofing Company crew before coming to Clemson. They would drive back and forth between Clemson and Sumter together in Kinard's malfunctioning old Volkswagen and formed half of an incomparable secondary in 1981.

Presbyterian and Wofford offered Rose scholarships out of high school, but he became convinced that he could succeed on a Division I-A team. Rose tagged along on visits to Clemson with Mayewood High School teammate Willis Carolina, a more highly recruited athlete who went to New Mexico Military Institute and later played for the New York Giants. Rose and Mayewood coach Rudy Wheeler became convinced Rose could play Division I-A football. Rose turned down the scholarship offers and walked on at Clemson.

Unlike Hall, who played a big role even early in his career though he, too, was a walk-on, Rose struggled at first. The process of proving oneself as a walk-on is thankless and nerve-wracking, and Rose was just about to quit when coach Danny Ford took him aside for a talk.

"Anthony Rose, I've been watching you," Rose remembers Ford saying. "You have some natural gifts and abilities. You need to keep working hard, and you're going to be a great Tiger one day. You're going to be a great football player one day. Don't give up."

To this day, Rose is impressed that Ford was in tune enough with his players to know that Rose was struggling at that time. He took Ford's advice and eventually became a sort of emotional leader and spokesman for the national championship team.

Rose admits that he has the gift of gab but hardly intended to be the team motivational speaker when he was first asked to speak in front of the team. But one day when he was given the chance, he fired up the Tigers so much that they asked him to talk again, and again, and again.

His speeches were fairly simple, sometimes focusing on the team mascots.

"It is unrealistic and not understandable in my mind that a Deacon could beat a Tiger," he would say. "So we've just got to go out and show what the Tigers are made of. We've worked hard. We've prepared. We've got the best talent in the country. We know what we're made of. Let's just go show it to everybody else."

On the field, Rose didn't have Hall's athletic ability, but he made up for it with a keen sense of positioning and comprehensive knowledge of the game plan. Hall would line up on what's considered the quarterback's strong side (toward the right of a right-handed cornerback), and Rose would take the other side of the field.

With Hall and Rose as the primary pass defenders along with talented backup cornerbacks Rod McSwain and Vandel Arrington, the Tigers never gave up a pass of more than 30 yards the whole season and held opponents to a completion percentage of .470. Rose said the effervescent Hall was a big reason for their success.

"He had a lot of confidence in his skills and abilities," Rose said, "and he even helped me with mine."

Defensive backs coach Curley Hallman used Hall and Rose as examples for years afterward in coaching. He would explain to his players that Hall and Rose were small guys who came to Clemson without scholarships and started on a national championship team.

"They had character, and they had good feet," Hallman said. "And when it comes right down to it, they were really smart football players. They understood everything you were trying to do and had really good knowledge of the scheme and were good leaders."

Strong safety Tim Childers was one of just three Clemson starters (excluding special teams) who wasn't a junior or senior.

"It was extremely important for me not to let my teammates down," Childers said. "I'm sure they felt the same way. Nobody wanted to let anybody down; but as an underclassman, you wanted to see the seniors leave on a good note."

Childers' career got off to an uncertain start. He married his wife, Donna, then briefly transferred to Appalachian State. He had played quarterback at Gaffney High School, then switched to defensive back.

Back at Clemson as a redshirt freshman in the fall of 1980, Childers played for the junior varsity. During practice, he studied senior strong safety Willie Underwood like an apprentice learning from a master.

Underwood made 69 tackles, led the team with eight passes broken up, intercepted two passes (both against South Carolina), and blocked a punt in a well-rounded senior season in 1980.

"As far as playing the position the way it was designed back then, he was a great player," Childers said, "and I thought if you could pattern a strong safety after anybody, it would be Willie Underwood."

Patterning his game after Underwood's made Childers an intense, physical player willing to do whatever his coaches asked. With a strong spring practice in 1981, he leaped out of obscurity to earn a starting position and make his biggest plays in the biggest games.

He made Clemson's only sack in the Orange Bowl for a 12-yard loss on third down. Against Georgia, he made a season-high nine tackles with one interception as the defending national champion managed just three points.

He made a diving catch of a tipped ball for an interception against South Carolina. Perhaps because of the way he got the job as a sophomore among so many upperclassmen, Childers especially treasures his position on that team.

"You would do anything for your teammates," he said. "That's the camaraderie I wish every athlete could experience. It was just one big, happy season for me, just being around that team."

The opening moments of games weren't always so pleasant for Childers, though.

Hallman said Childers used to get so excited that he would get the dry heaves on the defense's first series and appear ready to faint on the field.

Fortunately, Clemson had a capable and willing substitute for Childers in Jeff Suttle, who made 38 tackles while Childers made 41 in 1981. Suttle was from Lafayette, Georgia, and got Hallman's attention in recruiting because of his ability to hit incredibly hard.

"He had a little bit of that meanness in him," Hallman said. "When he had a chance to hit you, he would hurt you. And there's nothing wrong with that. I didn't say he was a dirty player. He had a little bit of a mean streak."

EXTRA POINTS ... AND HOME RUNS

Bob Paulling blames the end of his school-record extra-point streak on the wind and the officials.

Paulling was 5-for-5 on extra-point attempts as a freshman in 1979 before redshirting in 1980. In 1981, he made his first 31 extra-point kicks to break the school record of 35 held by Lon Armstrong.

The 37th kick, against South Carolina, was the strangest one of the season. The wind was blowing left to right, and Paulling kicked off a tee, so he launched the ball high above the top of the upright.

According to Paulling, the wind pushed the ball off to the right, but not until it went through the uprights. The official didn't see it that way and called it no good. Paulling didn't realize it until he was running off the field.

"You're kidding me," he called out to the official.

The referee told him the kick was wide right. To this day, Paulling disputes the call and is certain the kick went through the uprights.

"I'm positive," he said. "I've even got it on videotape. The game was televised, and I have a camera shot from the end zone."

Paulling didn't miss another extra-point attempt until his senior season against South Carolina two years later. The timing on that kick was thrown off because Clemson was using a substitute long snapper, Paulling said.

When Paulling was a freshman, his American Legion team from Orangeburg was in the playoffs as Clemson's fall football practice began.

Coach Danny Ford allowed Paulling to miss the afternoon sessions during two-a-days so he could compete with his Legion team in the regional playoffs.

"I'm sure it would be an exception to the rule," Paulling said of Ford's willingness to allow him to miss practice, "but again, being a kicker was a little unique."

Though Ford was a demanding coach, he wasn't totally opposed to his players competing in other sports at Clemson. Billy Davis, the punt returner on the 1981 team, played baseball—though not until 1983. Chuck and Rod McSwain ran for the track team.

In the fall of 1981, Ford's place-kicker was Nigerian Donald Igwebuike, whom Ford recruited from coach I.M. Ibrahim's soccer team. Igwebuike also played midfield for the Clemson soccer team, scoring twice in a victory over South Carolina.

Paulling was a successful baseball player, with a career batting average of .339 as a first baseman and outfielder. He participated in spring football practice and still managed to bat cleanup for most of the 1980 season, hitting .303 and finishing second on the team in RBIs.

"They didn't have a problem with it," Paulling said of the football coaches.

Using two-sport athletes helped Clemson get the best players on the football field, and that was the bottom line.

TOUGH GUYS ... TRIPLETT AND REMBERT

Jeff Davis deservedly gets most of the publicity from Clemson's linebacking corps that season, but Danny Triplett and backup Johnny Rembert were significant contributors, too.

Dan Benish, Triplett's roommate, said Triplett made an impression on his teammates the moment he introduced himself as a freshman.

"My name is Danny Triplett, from Boone, North Carolina," Triplett announced, and teammates snickered because of the country twang in his voice.

Triplett saved some of his best performances for the biggest games with 11 tackles against Georgia to earn ACC defensive lineman of the week honors, and 11 against North Carolina. He caused a Nebraska fumble on the opening possession of the Orange Bowl that set the tone for the game.

In practice, it didn't take long for his teammates to stop snickering at him, because he hit them just as hard as Clemson's opponents.

"He was tough as nails," said linebacker coach Les Herrin. "In practice or any time, if he had that shot, he was going to take it."

Johnny Rembert was the top backup at linebacker, a transfer from Cowley County Junior College in Kansas with tremendous natural ability. He was used more in passing situations because of his coverage ability and ran the 40-yard dash in 4.7 seconds, one of the fastest times on the team for non-backs.

The highlight of Rembert's 10-year NFL career with the New England Patriots was his selection to the Pro Bowl and All-Pro team in 1988.

"He had great talent," Herrin said, "and I think what really helped Johnny was Jeff being in there and being such a solid person."

FIRING UP THE TROOPS

One of the championship team's favorite rituals occurred after the team meal on Friday nights, when the players went to the movies.

On the bus, either on the way to the theater or on the way back to the hotel, players started chanting, "Patton, Patton." It became a chorus, and soon the whole team would be shouting "Patton, Patton."

Anthony Parete, the reserve quarterback who held the ball on extra points and field goal attempts, would make his way to the front of the bus. Parete had memorized George C. Scott's famous opening speech from the 1970 movie *Patton*, an account of General George Patton's command during World War II.

"I want you to remember that no man ever won a war by dying for his country," Parete would shout. "He won it by making the other poor, dumb [soldier] die for his country."

Parete had the entire speech and Scott's mannerisms memorized.

The speech, given to Patton's soldiers during the movie, was full of sports references. The general told his troops that they admired big league ball players and boxers, that they loved winners and wouldn't tolerate losers. He told them that the army lives, eats, sleeps, and fights as a team.

Parete delivered the speech tongue in cheek, and it was funny because, despite all the references to football as war, the players knew there was a big difference. At the same time, the messages of teamwork and what it takes to win were worthwhile on the eve of a game.

"It's pretty hilarious when you take it out of context like that and use it on a bus full of football players," Parete said. "It was inspiring, too."

Parete also often had fun on the bus at the expense of teammate James Farr, an offensive guard who grew up on a farm in Georgia and spoke with a distinctive country drawl. It didn't take long for the entire offensive line to join in with impressions of Farr.

"He would mock me and talk like me," Farr said of Parete, "and they would start getting in with him and start trying to talk like me as well, because I've got a Southern accent more so than a lot of them did."

Farr, a quiet, reserved underclassman, didn't take offense. His teammates were having fun; and he was, too.

Clemson's trips to the movie theater also were famous for the tricks wide receiver Perry Tuttle's teammates played on him.

Jerry Gaillard, Mark Richardson, and Jeff Stockstill would hide behind the curtains of the movie theater in Anderson once it got dark and jump out to scare Tuttle. The high-strung Tuttle would run out of the theater screaming.

"He was like a cat on a hot tin roof all the time," Parete said. "He was jumpy. ... Poor Tuttle. They would just harass that guy."

5

AHEAD OF ITS TIME:
Clemson's Foundation for Success

❝ The IPTAY people in every county were competing—Greenville would beat Spartanburg—whatever. There was a lot of competition in getting members to join IPTAY, and they had a lot of input and a lot of insight. **❞**

– Athletics director Bill McLellan

A diabetic lady approached Clemson athletics director Bill McLellan one day with a request.

She attended games at Death Valley and could only purchase sugary sodas at the concession stands. She needed something sugar free to quench her thirst.

"I can remember putting the diet drinks in at that request," McLellan said, "and of course, before long, most of the drinks were diet."

Dating back to the 1930s, Clemson athletics was ahead of its time in almost every respect, right down to the soft drinks it served.

Clemson's success building an infrastructure to support football played a huge role in the formation of a national championship program.

In 1934, Dr. Rupert Fike started IPTAY, the fundraising group whose acronym stood for "I Pay Ten A Year." It was the forerunner of the athletics booster organizations that support virtually every college program today.

Personal seat licenses are viewed as a relatively new way of athletics funding, but IPTAY was a model with a similar concept that began more than 70 years ago with a total contribution of $1,600. Boosters paid a set fee for the right to purchase season tickets [by 1981, IPTAY stood for "I Pay Thirty A Year"]. In the beginning, even goods such as sweet potatoes and turnip greens were accepted as school officials sought to build membership. The money IPTAY collected went directly to fund scholarships for athletes. In 1980-81, IPTAY collected $3 million for the first time, with more than 16,000 members contributing.

IPTAY's board of regional directors wielded considerable influence on athletics department affairs. IPTAY also helped the athletics department officials stay connected to Clemson graduates who could help their school do things cheaper whether Clemson needed concrete to build columns for the stadium or sod to cover the field.

"They had a lot of input and a lot of insight," McLellan said. "We took it all to the IPTAY board [when a project needed to get done]. I think the IPTAY board helped us. They had a lot of foresight."

As early as the 1950s, Clemson kept its athletics facilities growing by adding a tax of 50 or 75 cents to each ticket to pay for improvements. McLellan credits Dr. R.C. Edwards with helping the school and athletics department build facilities that were among the finest in the nation at the time. Edwards, perhaps Clemson's greatest president ever, served from 1958-79. Edwards was a businessman, having worked for Deering-Milliken after serving in the Army, and McLellan said he possessed a financial acumen that some college presidents who advance through academia lack.

McLellan, who became athletics director in 1971, worked with Edwards to overcome significant obstacles as Clemson changed rapidly during the 1970s. Women were first admitted to Clemson in 1955, and the athletics program began accommodating them by building Jervey Athletic Center to house 12 men's and seven women's sports programs in the early 1970s.

Memorial Stadium also grew, from 58,000 seats to 63,000 in 1981. "We had to [expand facilities]," McLellan said. "Clemson was growing."

It took unorthodox financing ideas to get many facilities projects off the ground. Death Valley was among the first college stadiums to have luxury boxes, which now are considered a staple of big-time athletics fund raising. McLellan got the first 26 built by telling boosters they could get in on these premium seats by purchasing for four years in advance. He threw in an extra free year for those boosters to get the project moving.

All this was important because Clemson was building a big-time atmosphere around a football program at a small-town school. In the late 1970s and early 1980s, few college stadiums had more than 60,000 seats, few had luxury boxes and few had office complexes comparable to Clemson's at Jervey.

The facilities and the financial health of a program whose scholarships were funded by IPTAY were two reasons Danny Ford was able to recruit so many top athletes to take the Tigers through an undefeated season.

STRUGGLES IN 1980

It took one gigantic turnaround to get Clemson the national title in 1981.

The 1980 season was a huge disappointment after the Tigers had built considerable momentum for the program under Charley Pell and then Ford. Pell took over in 1977 and had impressive talent at his disposal courtesy of the previous coach, Red Parker. Parker recruited Steve Fuller, Jerry Butler, and Dwight Clark, but went 17-27-2 over four seasons.

Pell showed immediately that he knew how to use all that talent. He led Clemson to an 8-3-1 record and a Gator Bowl appearance in 1977, the Tigers' first postseason appearance since 1959.

"His personality around the players ... he had their complete attention," McLellan said.

In 1978, Clemson was 10-1 when Pell left for Florida. Pell died of cancer in 2001, and players and former Clemson assistants say he didn't think he could win a national title at Clemson. McLellan and the Clemson administration picked Ford to replace Pell, and that helped keep several key members of the staff in place. Defensive ends coach Willie Anderson, offensive tackles coach Buddy King, and running backs coach Chuck Reedy all stayed on the staff with Ford, who had been Pell's assistant head coach, and coached the offensive line along with King.

"When he left he said he'd come back and talk to all of us, but he never did," Reedy said.

Reedy said it might have bothered offensive coordinator Jimmye Laycock a bit that Pell didn't at least offer him a job. Laycock stayed around for another year under Ford before leaving to coach for a quarter-century at his alma mater, William & Mary.

Still, Reedy is convinced all the coaches were better off under Ford.

"Coach Pell was very, very difficult to work for," Reedy said. "I had no desire to go with him. I doubt Jimmye or the other guys would have gone, either."

Ford immediately demonstrated that he could be a successful head coach. With Pell gone, Ford directed the Tigers in the Gator Bowl against Ohio State. Clemson won 17-15 as Ohio State coach Woody Hayes punched Clemson middle guard Charlie Bauman after he was forced out of bounds on the Ohio State sideline following a fourth-quarter interception. Ohio State ended Hayes' career after that incident, but Ford's career appeared to be off to a good start.

In Ford's first full season, the Tigers went 8-4 with a loss to Baylor in the Peach Bowl, the team's third-straight bowl appearance. Clemson appeared to regress just a bit, losing 19-0 at home to Maryland, but still kept fans happy with a 16-10 victory at Notre Dame in one of just two games the school has played against the nation's most storied program.

Then, in 1980, just about everything seemed to go wrong.

"We just didn't have the continuity we had the year before," said Clemson defensive tackle Dan Benish. "It was tough."

In the second game of the season, Clemson lost 20-16 to the eventual national champion, Georgia, despite outgaining the Bulldogs 351 yards to 157. Scott Woerner set the tone for many Clemson losses that season when he returned a punt 67 yards for a touchdown and an interception 98 yards to set up another score in the first quarter.

Three times that season, opponents used multiple big returns to score or set up scores Clemson's competent defense couldn't stop. When the Tigers lost 34-17 to Duke, Dennis Tabron intercepted three passes, returning one 87 yards for a score and setting up a touchdown with another.

That was a humbling defeat for Clemson, which was 11-1 against Duke from 1977 to 1988. Quarterback Homer Jordan remembers getting booed that day, which happened to be Parents' Day at Memorial Stadium. The players understood. They didn't believe they should ever lose to Duke.

"The football pride wasn't there at Duke like it was at Clemson University," said Clemson tight end Bubba Diggs. "It was just one of those times that we just didn't take care of business."

The next week brought more of the same, as North Carolina State turned a fumble, interception, safety, and blocked punt into 21 points in a 24-20 victory. The Tigers limped into the season finale with a 5-5 record, and there was all sorts of grumbling about the team.

Though McLellan has said he was fully behind Ford, Reedy said the staff members were afraid they would get fired if Clemson didn't defeat South Carolina in the season finale. Worse yet, there were rumors that there was racial tension on the team.

"They talked about us having some racial issues, which was so far off base that it wasn't even true," said wide receiver Jerry Gaillard.

ORANGE BRITCHES

By pulling this team together for the South Carolina game with a memorable bit of motivation, Ford demonstrated that he was plenty capable of coaching a winning team.

He and equipment manager Len Gough had conspired to order orange pants for the team, and Ford used them to motivate the players. At breakfast the morning of the game, the players didn't have a clue what Ford had in store for them.

Punt returner Billy Davis remembers players looking around at one another nervously as Ford asked for their attention.

"Y'all listen up," Davis remembered Ford saying. "I've got something to tell you."

Davis was afraid Ford might announce he was resigning after the game. Instead, Len Gough brought a box over to him.

"We are wearing orange britches today," he told the players, "and we don't lose in orange britches."

The players went wild with excitement. They warmed up in their white pants, then changed into orange and boarded the buses to carry them around the outside of the stadium at the hill for their big entrance. The fans went nuts.

"We had never seen anything like that, and we were going wild," said defensive end Bill Smith. "So from that point on, it never even crossed our mind that we were going to lose that game."

South Carolina had Heisman Trophy winner George Rogers at tailback and finished 8-4 that season. But the Gamecocks were no match for Clemson in that electric, orange-loving environment.

Rogers rushed for 168 yards on 28 carries, but finished his four-year career without a touchdown against Clemson. Tigers safety Willie Underwood made the biggest impact of the game with one of the most memorable performances in the history of the storied series.

With the score tied 6-6 in the third quarter, Underwood intercepted Gary Harper and returned 64 yards to set up a 1-yard touchdown run by Homer Jordan. Three plays later, Underwood intercepted Harper again, returning 37 yards for a touchdown.

Though Underwood's final game as a senior was memorable, his understudy, Tim Childers, considered it a shame that Underwood didn't get to play for the national championship team.

"He was extremely tough," Childers said. "I feel sorry for Willie that he didn't have that one more year of eligibility. That was unfortunate for him, but it was fortunate for me."

Ford celebrated after the game by dancing on tables in the locker room as he sang to his players. After defeating South Carolina, it was a Clemson tradition to sing the Cockadoodledoo Song:

"Cockadoodledoo," Ford crowed. "Cockadoodledoo. Carolina Gamecocks, the [heck] with you."

The victory and the motivational move with the jerseys gave fans something to talk about in the off-season and had the players feeling upbeat about the future.

"We needed something to springboard us into the next year," said defensive tackle William Devane.

That win built anticipation heading into the summer, and the seniors capitalized on that. Jeff Davis, Perry Tuttle, Lee Nanney, and others demanded that players show up for summer weightlifting sessions that were supposed to be voluntary.

George Dostal, the strength training coach, set the Orange Bowl as a goal.

"They started putting up orange pictures and things like that in the weight room," said quarterback Homer Jordan. "That's what I remember. They painted that picture for us, and we started visualizing being in the Orange Bowl, playing in the national championship game."

'THE JUDGE' AND PERRY'S GREATEST HITS

A special camaraderie was building among the players. Meanwhile, sports information assistant Kim Kelly was coming up with ways to market the players that would gain them national attention once the season began.

Jeff Davis' initials rattled around in Kelly's head before the season as she tried to think of a way to promote him for All-America.

This photo of Jeff Davis as "The Judge" was part of Clemson's marketing campaign that helped him earn first-team All-America honors.

J.D. Judge of the Defense. The Judge. That was it. That was how she was going to do it.

Kelly started working in 1980 as the first full-time female in Clemson's sports information department. Her specialty was promotions.

Bob Bradley, the late, legendary sports information director who made Frank Howard a household name, was famous for making writers and broadcasters feel at home with his homespun Southern charm. Tim Bourret, who would later take over for Bradley, worked in the office and was a whiz with statistics.

Kelly was the creative genius in the department. She was the one who could get the most interesting details from players for the profile stories she wrote for game programs. Most strikingly, she found unusual ways to promote the players long before the Bobblehead dolls and artistic gimmicks used today became terribly clichéd.

Clemson gave Kelly enough of a budget to promote two players during the summer of 1981. Davis, who led the ACC in 1980 with 160 tackles, and his roommate, Perry Tuttle, who had a school-record 915 receiving yards in 1980, were chosen.

Davis was perfect for Kelly's "Judge" concept. He was the unquestioned leader of the defense, judge and jury for teammates whom he forcefully corrected when they made mistakes. He wasn't especially outgoing, but rather had a quiet confidence that made him appear almost regal. Former Clemson player Walter Cox III, a Pickens County Court judge, arranged to allow Davis to use his courtroom and robe. Kelly settled on making black and white posters of Davis to send to media members who would vote for All-America. Black and white was less expensive than color and would reproduce well in newspapers that picked up on the promotion.

A creative, personable young photographer named Lance McKinney set up the shoot in the courtroom. He asked Davis to bang on the gavel. Davis, who wasn't afraid to run full force into huge men wearing helmets and pads, timidly tapped the gavel.

McKinney told Davis he knew he had more personality than that. Davis banged the gavel hard, then smiled and loosened up.

"It got quiet," Kelly said. "There were people around the courthouse that knew this was happening. Then there were people that didn't know what was happening, looking in to see what this was all about."

Kelly was listening to music on some old, vinyl records, staring at a Teddy Pendergrass album when she thought up an idea for Tuttle. His promotion would center on the records he was breaking at Clemson. Kelly decided to make a fake album cover featuring Tuttle.

McKinney, who was good with props, gathered some albums and broke them for the cover. Tuttle, always comfortable in the limelight, took great care choosing the clothes he would wear on his "album cover." He settled on an orange-striped shirt with blue trim and blue drawstring dress pants.

"Perry Tuttle: The Record Breaker. An All-America Candidate. Cast Your Vote Now," the fake album cover read. The back cover listed his "greatest hits"—accomplishments on the field—as if they were songs.

The album cover and the judge poster were mailed to local media outlets and newspapers across the nation with circulations of 100,000 or more. Kelly said the players obviously needed to take care of their business on the field to become All-Americans, which they did. Davis made 175 tackles that season, and Tuttle caught 52 passes for 883 yards and eight touchdowns. Both were named first-team All-Americans in 1981.

There is no doubt in Kelly's mind that the promotions helped. The promotions generated publicity from reporters who asked the players what it was like to pose for such fun gimmicks. Kelly also is convinced the flashy materials caught the attention of All-America voters in other regions.

"It helps," Kelly said. "You have to have the ability. You have to have the talent. If they are doing well, and they're the type of individual that will have fun with that and will give something special, which they were and they did—it can work."

Kelly said Ed Wiley, a Clemson graduate and salesperson for Washburn Graphics in Charlotte, did a great job making the promotions look good. The company received PICA (Printing Industry of the Carolinas) awards for the product. Kelly's creativity paid off for her just as it did for the players. She received CoSida (College Sports Information Directors Association) awards for promotional pieces—a highly appreciated honor in a sports information department that reached a fevered pitch as the Tigers continued to win. Bradley would arrive a bit late to the office in the mornings because he would drive to the post office to pick up the newspapers. His assistants and student workers would pounce eagerly on the papers when they arrived, excited to see what had been written about Clemson that day.

"Everybody would be chomping at the bit to clip the papers," Kelly said. "You'd clip 'em out and stack 'em up, and people would file all the clips."

Bradley loved every minute. He would deflect attention to Kelly for the promotions and Bourret for finding meaningful statistics, but he entertained the media personally. As the Tigers kept winning and the story grew bigger, Bradley charmed reporters from more prestigious media outlets. Writers from *Sports Illustrated* and city newspapers such as Atlanta, Charlotte, Dallas and Philadelphia came to Clemson and got a full dose of South Carolina charm when they went out with Bradley.

Every Friday evening before home games, Bradley took visiting media to eat at Lonny's 93 Fish Camp on South Carolina-Route 93 near campus. The menu was always the same: catfish, hush puppies, cole slaw, and sweet tea. Bradley had to show Kelly how to eat catfish holding it by the tail. She said he would lean his head back, dangle the fish in his mouth and strip the meat from the bones with his teeth.

"It would be like a comic book, like in a cartoon," Kelly said.

Kelly keeps many of her promotional materials from her short time at Clemson to this day. She went on to do marketing for fast food restaurants, hospitals, and national health organizations, but never had as much fun as she did at Clemson. Years later, at Tuttle's 40th birthday party, Kelly was talking to some of the players about her time at Clemson.

They told her they thought that because she held such a high-powered job in the athletics department, she was a lot older than they were. Not so. She had just graduated from St. Mary's College in South Bend, Indiana, where she had worked in the sports information department at neighboring University of Notre Dame.

She looks back on her time at Clemson as one of the most pleasant experiences of her life.

"It was just a whirlwind. I probably got almost all my 15 minutes of fame in those three years at Clemson," she said. "It was delightful to be able to promote people and connect with and write about real people making a contribution toward a team effort that turned out so wonderfully."

As Kelly designed her clever advertising campaigns for Davis and Tuttle, the team was growing closer together in the intense summer workouts designed by Dostal. Their minds were filled with images of the Orange Bowl.

Their hearts were filled with anguish over a season gone bad in 1980. Coaches often say revenge is a faulty method of inspiration, but in this case Clemson's eagerness to get back at Georgia, Duke, and

North Carolina in particular caused the players to work harder during the off-season.

The players arrived at the 1981 season with an unranked team and players who had built excellent team chemistry because the off-season workout regimen was tremendously successful.

"We knew we were a better team than what we had shown," Jordan said.

They were about to prove it—in a big way.

6

TIDE TESTED:
A Defense-Oriented Game Plan

" We didn't have a lot of super, super players, but good, hardworking guys that believed in each other. It was just amazing. We'd get in the huddle and look at Jeff Davis; we'd look at each other; and we didn't want to screw it up. Nobody wanted to let the other person down. **"**

—Defensive tackle Dan Benish

The 1981 team was built according to classic football wisdom true to Ford's roots in Bear Bryant's revered Alabama program.

A stout defense and a superb kicking game were complemented by a ball-control offense that churned out yards with fullback dives, sweeps, and option plays, and hit opponents for big plays in the passing game when defenders crept too close to the line of scrimmage.

"We had a great defense, and we had an offense that, when they needed to score they would score," said defensive end Bill Smith. "They didn't turn the ball over, and we had great kickers. Even today, that's a great formula to win football games."

The defense was strong up front with sophomore William Devane and freshman William Perry sharing the nose tackle spot and senior Jeff Bryant, a second-team All-American, playing right tackle. Jeff Davis, one of the greatest and most inspirational players in Clemson history, anchored the linebacking corps. Junior free safety Terry Kinard, the only member of the team in the College Football Hall of Fame in South Bend, Indiana, prevented opponents from breaking free for big gains as leader of the secondary.

"With Terry back there roaming, he could cover so much ground, it wasn't necessary for us to play man to man," said strong safety Tim Childers. "Very few quarterbacks we came up against were able to pick us apart."

Childers estimates that Clemson used zone pass defense schemes about 80 percent of the time. Neither offenses nor defenses were as diverse or complex as they are now, and Clemson kept its schemes simple. The Tigers' basic zone had the two corners and Kinard each responsible for one-third of the field, with Childers and the linebackers covering the flats.

Clemson blitzed a lot, and opposing quarterbacks suffered as a result. Eight times that season, the Tigers had at least four sacks.

"I give a lot of credit to the defensive schemes that were run up front," said cornerback Anthony Rose. "They put just a tremendous amount of pressure on the offensive line and the quarterback."

DEPENDENT ON DEFENSE

The Tigers ranked second in the nation in scoring defense, allowing just 8.2 points per game, and didn't allow a rushing touchdown until the seventh game of the season, against North Carolina State.

Opponents gained just 251.5 yards per game against the Tigers. Clemson's offense, grounded in Ford's conservative principles, was more modestly successful. In three of the first four games, Clemson failed to gain more than 280 yards.

Nonetheless, the players on offense never would have admitted the defense's superiority. That would have been admitting defeat because the units competed ferociously during practice.

"Back then, we thought the offense was better than the defense," said center Tony Berryhill.

The tension between the two units probably made everybody better but teetered on the verge of creating destructive ill will. The players on defense were the instigators and the more fluent trash talkers. Defensive coordinator Tom Harper purposely fostered playing-field arrogance bordering on obnoxious.

That was fun during games when the Tigers were whipping up on opponents—it wasn't so much fun during practice for the offense.

"When the No. 1 defense had to go against the No. 1 offense during practice, I hated it, not because I thought they were a better team and a better side and were physical," said wide receiver Perry Tuttle. "It was just that they jawed all the time and talked more trash than anybody I ever knew."

Tuttle said he was one of the few players on offense who overcame his disgust from practice to hang out with people from the defense. He got to know Harper well and roomed with linebacker Jeff Davis.

He gained respect for how the defense was coached and how it performed.

"They were so well prepared at game day," Tuttle said. "They felt they knew the game plan so well, and to be quite honest with you, it rubbed off on the offensive side of the ball."

Harper, who handled the defensive line, coached to players' strengths and didn't ask them to do anything beyond their capabilities. Jeff Bryant was incredibly athletic, so Harper turned him loose to rush the passer on almost every play.

Dan Benish was one of the most cerebral players on the team, and Harper allowed him to make calls for the defensive linemen. Ordinarily, the linebackers would have made those calls, but Benish's brains made it possible for them to concentrate on their own assignments.

Harper's willingness to delegate decision making to his players was remarkable for a college coach. Sometimes he didn't know what calls had been made on the field until he watched film the following week. His confidence made them more self-assured and aggressive, and that helped them dominate.

"He brought us all together," Benish said. "We had a solid defensive front. He helped give us that swagger we needed, and it was just awesome."

DAVIS' DOMINATION

The defense was designed to funnel a lot of traffic to the linebackers, and one player in particular would be remembered as one of the best in Clemson history.

Senior weak side linebacker Jeff Davis was a superior leader who demanded that every player on the team pull his own weight.

"Jeff Davis was the leader of our team without question," Childers said. "Ninety-nine percent of the people you talk to would agree with that."

Davis also played his position as well as any linebacker Clemson has ever had. With the powerful defensive linemen often occupying more than one blocker apiece, Davis often roamed free to zero in on opposing running backs.

He was fast enough to chase them from sideline to sideline, and his legs were like tree trunks. Davis made 175 tackles in 1981, setting a school record that stood until Anthony Simmons made 178 in 1996.

The strong side linebacker, Danny Triplett, wasn't as athletic or productive as Davis and didn't run free as much because he lined up over the tight end. Triplett's contribution was a recklessness that inspired his teammates to increase their intensity on the field.

"He always walked around like he was dazed," said Benish, who was Triplett's roommate. "He brought it. He had no regard for his body."

Andy Headen, a converted quarterback, played the "bandit" position, a hybrid between a defensive end and an outside linebacker. He made four tackles behind the line of scrimmage that season and dropped back in coverage to rank second to cornerback Hollis Hall with eight broken-up passes.

Clemson's defensive backs didn't have to cover for long periods because the front seven created incredible pressure. Hall and Anthony Rose were former walk-ons at cornerback who played with confidence bordering on cockiness and seldom got burned deep. The longest pass by an opponent that season was 30 yards, and Clemson intercepted 23 passes while allowing just six touchdown passes.

As the last line of defense, Kinard seldom let anybody get behind him. He closed on the ball quickly, making a team-high six interceptions.

"He was quick, and he was fast," said wide receiver Frank Magwood. "He had, I guess, a nose for the football. He always seemed to know where the football was. I guess it's instinct, playing that position. He was really good."

From back with Kinard to front with Bryant, this defense was ahead of its time because of its emphasis on speed. The great Miami teams of the 1980s under Jimmy Johnson are credited with creating the fascination with speed rather than strength that survives to this day. Under Ford, Clemson's defense in 1981 was an earlier prototype of a defense built on speed.

"We were never worried about the defense doing their job," said quarterback Homer Jordan, "because we always knew they would."

THE FOUR-YARD RULE

The simple genius of the offense started up front, fittingly for a team whose head coach formerly coached the offensive line. Clemson used man-blocking schemes almost exclusively and was content to run until the opponent proved it could stop the run.

Ford demanded that each of his offensive linemen knock his man five yards back from the line of scrimmage.

"If you drove him five yards off the ball and the ball carrier was behind you, you gained four yards," said center Tony Berryhill. "And [Ford's] thing was, if on the first two downs you gained 4 yards a down, you were third-and-two, and it was a lot easier to get a first down."

Five yards were demanded of the offensive linemen. Four yards were demanded of the backs. Tailback Chuck McSwain said Ford didn't care much about breakaway plays—20- or 30-yard runs. But if you fell short of 4 yards on many of your carries, you wouldn't stay in the game long as a running back.

After the season, McSwain said, pro scouts wanted to know why he and fellow tailback Cliff Austin didn't break more long runs.

"That was mainly because [Ford] was more concerned about getting it up in there and going straight up the field, not trying to make the spectacular run," McSwain said.

Ford prepared the backs to get those 4 yards by making the resistance in practice greater than anything the offense would face in a game. They already were lining up against one of the best defenses in the nation. Ford made it more difficult on the offense by telling the defense which play was coming, still demanding 4 yards on the runs.

"It was just to toughen you up," McSwain said.

For the record, the Tigers averaged 4.2 yards per carry that season. Tailbacks Austin (5.1) and McSwain (4.8) and fullback Jeff McCall (4.8) all were well over 4 yards per carry.

Clemson's running game was solid even though its backs might not have measured up to the talent of some of the teams the Tigers faced in the national championship season.

Georgia had Herschel Walker, one of the greatest college running backs of all time, who would win the Heisman Trophy in 1982 as the nation's best college player. Nebraska had 1983 Heisman winner Mike Rozier and Roger Craig, who in 1985 with the San Francisco 49ers became the first back in NFL history to have 1,000 yards rushing and 1,000 yards receiving in the same season.

All the Tigers did was win the national title without any single player rushing for over 824 yards. They had two fullbacks and two tailbacks sharing playing time and carries and powering a rushing attack that averaged 248.1 yards per game.

At fullback, Jeff McCall and Kevin Mack possessed different skills that were useful at different points in the game. Mack was fast enough to outrun safeties if he got into the secondary; he later rushed for more than 1,000 yards for the Cleveland Browns in 1985.

McCall was a stronger, more physical runner, and almost certain not to fumble.

"A lot of times I knew in tight game situations, Coach [Chuck] Reedy would be more likely to put me in there," McCall said. "I wasn't going to fumble, and he knew not to expect any mistakes."

McCall rushed for 457 yards on 96 carries, and Mack carried 76 times for 287 yards. They played a position of incredible importance in a rushing-oriented offense. Their tough running up the gut forced the defense to collapse inside, opening the corners for Jordan on keepers and Austin and McSwain on the pitch.

The fullbacks' blocking against the linebackers on lead plays often determined whether the tailback would get a decent gain. The one constant, McCall said, was physical punishment, whether tacklers were beating on them or the fullbacks were initiating contact with their blocks. He didn't mind sharing time with Mack. At times, he welcomed a break.

"It's good to have somebody in relief as a backup," McCall said. "You're either hitting or getting hit every play."

TAILBACKING IN TANDEM

McSwain said he and Austin alternated series each game, and McSwain preferred to let Austin go first. McSwain believed that many times, the offense goes three downs and then punts on the first series as it gets adjusted to working against an unfamiliar defense.

The other reason was that McSwain preferred to watch how the defense reacted to Austin before going into the game himself.

"If we'd run a sweep I could see if I could run it inside or outside," McSwain said. "I'd just say, 'Cliff, go ahead and start, and I'll just take the next series.' I could sit on the sideline and watch what was going on, and that would help me."

Clemson's pairings of McCall with Austin and Mack with McSwain had a strategic purpose, according to Reedy, who coached the running backs. Austin and Mack were the better blockers, so Clemson wanted one of them on the field at all times. In 1981, Clemson instituted a series of plays from the "Offset-I" formation, where the fullback didn't line up directly behind the tailback.

That allowed the tailback to block for the fullback and helped Clemson take advantage of Austin's blocking ability, in particular, when McCall was running. Clemson also called certain plays at certain times to play to the strengths of the particular backs in the game. For instance, they preferred to run the inside veer off the option when Mack was in the game because his quickness made him especially dangerous on the play.

"All four of them could do everything," Reedy said. "But there were certain combinations that you liked a little bit better."

The thing that impressed Reedy most about all four backs was their unselfishness. Heading into the Orange Bowl, it was decided that a coin toss would determine which tailback would start. McSwain won the coin toss, but again deferred to Austin. It's a rare football player who would turn down a chance to start in a game to decide the national championship. McSwain decided that, since having Austin start had worked all season, there was no sense changing the substitution pattern for the bowl game.

Despite the camaraderie in the backfield, it was human nature for all the backs to wish they had more prominent roles.

"Other running backs at the time were getting 1,000 yards, 1,200 yards," McSwain said.

"We always wondered what it would be like if we got 25, 30 carries a game."

They had to be satisfied with 10 to 12 carries.

Austin was a bigger back than McSwain with a straight-ahead burst but decreased quickness after having knee surgery to repair an injury suffered in the 1979 spring game. Austin showed flashes of brilliance and dazzling speed as a freshman in 1978, when he was the third-team tailback but scored the winning points in the Gator Bowl against Ohio State on a 1-yard run. Austin redshirted in 1979 and was ineffective and still not completely healed in 1980.

Finally, in 1981, Austin regained his swagger, though his yards came more as a result of toughness than blinding speed. McSwain was quicker and shiftier and demonstrated his skills with a 25-carry, 151-yard performance against South Carolina when Austin was injured during the game.

It was Clemson's second-largest rushing total in any game that season, one of just four 100-yard games by the Tiger backs that season.

JORDAN RULES

Another key to the success of the offense was quarterback Homer Jordan, an often underappreciated player because he was more quiet and unassuming than other team leaders such as Jeff Davis and Perry Tuttle. Jordan was a wiry 6 feet and 175 pounds and more elusive than a greased chicken in a barnyard.

He also was familiar with the offense because it was identical to the one he ran at Cedar Shoals High School in Athens, Georgia. Jordan almost was switched to cornerback during the spring of his junior year, when he played a few snaps in the spring game at that position.

But he had enough passing ability to beat out the athletic Andy Headen—a superb option quarterback—for the starting position that fall. Jordan's impact on the team couldn't be measured in yards or touchdowns.

"He had the trust of all the players around him because they knew what type of person he was," said Nelson Stokley, who coached the quarterbacks. "The players kind of fed off him. He did everything right. He didn't take any shortcuts."

Jordan understood that on a team built around a superior defense, one of his top responsibilities was to protect the football.

"We were never worried about the defense doing their job, because we always knew they would," Jordan said. "'We can't turn the ball over as an offense, was how we were thinking."

Ford had difficulty letting go of the idea that Headen could be his quarterback. *Sports Illustrated* named Headen Clemson's top recruit in his class, and he was incredibly gifted as a runner. He had the speed to outrun opposing defensive backs and the size at 6 feet, 5 inches, and 230 pounds to run them over.

In the 1980 spring game, he completed 10-of-18 passes for 178 yards. He threw two touchdown passes, led his team to three touchdowns in the final six minutes, and was named the starting quarterback afterward. His success as a passer turned out to be an aberration. In the fall, he wasn't accurate enough to keep the defense from loading up against the run at the line of scrimmage.

"He had a great arm," Stokley said, "but he missed some things in putting the touch on the football."

Headen played quarterback briefly in the 1980 opener against Rice, but separated his shoulder. When he came back four games later, he had been moved to defense.

Clemson also had Mike Gasque, who was an accurate pocket passer, and he shared time with Jordan in 1980. Jordan wasn't as good a passer as Gasque, and he wasn't as dynamic a runner as Headen. Jordan performed both skills—running and passing—well enough to be the best dual-threat quarterback on the team.

Ford talked to Jordan about the historical significance of Jordan getting the job after naming him the starter. Jordan was about to be the first black starting quarterback at Clemson, and in the South that was bound to stir racial tensions.

Ford told Jordan that he'd better be good, because if he wasn't, both Jordan and Ford would hear about it. Jordan performed well enough that neither of them experienced a lot of questioning on the racial issue.

"I didn't think there was really much to it because he was such a good person and such a great leader that the other people really rallied around him," Stokley said. "It's the type of person he was. He was able to handle that extremely well, and he played extremely well."

Headen switched to defense, where he played the bandit outside linebacker/end position. He made 53 tackles and knocked a Nebraska desperation pass to the turf on the final play of the Orange Bowl to clinch the national title for the Tigers.

After Headen's senior season, New York Giants coach Bill Parcells came to Clemson to talk to the staff about him. Stokley wondered whether Headen would fit into Parcells' system, but Parcells assured him he would.

Headen became an eighth-round draft choice of the Giants and played six seasons in the NFL, winning a Super Bowl ring in 1986.

"The best thing that happened is when I sat down and talked to him and he went over to [defense]," Stokley said. "... It certainly helped him, making that move. It wasn't an easy decision, but we also had a guy there, if anything happened he could come back and help us because he knew what was going on."

OPTION SOMETIMES PAINFUL

Clemson never needed Headen on offense. Jordan was much smaller, but was more of a slippery, elusive runner than Headen and a constant threat to break a big play on an option keeper.

That doesn't mean he liked running the option.

"Some teams, they didn't care if I had the ball or not, they were going to take the quarterback out," Jordan said. "It wasn't one of your favorite plays to run because you would probably get hit every play."

Jordan said he was fortunate to have a superior offensive line that often prevented him from being hit hard. One of the hardest hits he ever took came courtesy of teammate Jeff Davis in a scrimmage.

When Jordan was running an option play down the line of scrimmage, Davis just about knocked him out.

"I tried to run the next play and was just kind of wobbling to the line," Jordan said. "He just said [to the team trainers], 'Y'all better come and get him, because he's not ready.'"

Davis teases Jordan about that hit to this day.

Jordan's reads on the option were simple, and he executed them well. If the tackle went upfield, he handed to the fullback. Otherwise, Jordan kept the ball and waited for the end to commit to him or the tailback. Jordan kept the ball and turned upfield if the end stuck with the tailback, but pitched if the end tried to take Jordan down.

Tailback Chuck McSwain said it was obvious that opposing defenses developed their game plans to encourage him to pitch the ball.

"They'd rather have Cliff and me running the ball," McSwain said.

When opposing defenses overloaded the line of scrimmage to stop the run, Jordan was a good enough passer to make them pay. Many option quarterbacks threw wobbly balls because passing was not their specialty. Jordan's passes were crisp and on target.

"He threw a tight spiral, a tight-spinning football that didn't wobble a whole lot," said wide receiver Frank Magwood. "It was very catchable."

In an era when the passing game wasn't as highly developed as it is today, Jordan completed a respectable 54.6 percent of his passes (107 for 196) in 1981. He threw nine touchdown passes and nine interceptions. His passing efficiency rating of 133.4 tied him for 12th in Division I-A that season.

Jordan's teammates appreciated how he distributed the ball as a passer. Game-breaking wide receiver Perry Tuttle usually got the ball if he was open. If Tuttle wasn't open, Jordan didn't force it to him.

"He wasn't favoring a particular receiver," Magwood said. "He just wanted to throw the ball where the open receiver was. I guess that's what I liked about him."

A FEARSOME LINE

Clemson's offensive linemen had a Jekyll-Hyde reputation that served them well on game days. Tackles Lee Nanney and Brad Fisher, in particular, almost frightened some of their teammates as kickoff approached.

"The big offensive linemen just flat out, they had a switch," said Anthony Parete, a reserve quarterback who held for the place-kickers. "Those guys were the nicest guys in the dorm and seeing them around [campus]. They had a switch. You'd flip that switch, and they'd go into game mode; and you'd better steer clear."

Senior right tackle Nanney gained the most notoriety on the Clemson offensive line because of his school-record, 525-pound bench press.

Offensive linemen seldom get much publicity because they don't score touchdowns, intercept passes, or sack the quarterback, but Nanney's pure strength got him attention during the championship season. The Spartanburg native won All-ACC honors for his contributions as a blocker in the bruising rushing attack.

"Lee was an excellent football player—very tough, very strong, very physical," said offensive line coach Larry Van Der Heyden.

Nanney might have been the most athletic player on a line stocked with hard-nosed players who made the most of their talent. Center Tony Berryhill made All-ACC and was the leader of the line from a tactical aspect.

In Clemson's man-blocking scheme, the Tigers called the play in the huddle but didn't know their blocking assignments until they reached the line of scrimmage. Berryhill would start a communication process that worked from the middle of the line to the outside.

"I'm talking to the guards; the guards are talking to the tackles; and the tackles are talking to the tight ends," Berryhill said.

Left tackle Fisher was in his second season as a starter and wasn't as physically talented as Nanney, but played with great effort and seldom made a mistake.

Van Der Heyden said right guard Brian Clark had a reputation for being soft when he entered Clemson, but had good size and mobility. He shed the "soft" label that season, and the staff gained confidence in him as the season went along.

James Farr, the sophomore left guard, might have been the most gritty player on the entire team. He was listed at 6 feet, 4 inches tall and 217 pounds, tiny for an interior lineman even in the early 1980s.

"He was probably the toughest 215-pound player I've ever coached," Van Der Heyden said. "He was a really tough, hard-nosed kid, a great kid—an old country kid that was a good football player."

He initially had been homesick and wanted to return home when he reported to Clemson in 1980, but stayed in school and earned the praise of his coaches because he worked so hard to overcome his lack of size. Barely 18 years old in his first game as a freshman, he moved to center and started the opener against Rice because of injuries.

Tight end Bubba Diggs didn't get the ball as much as he hoped in the passing game. Clemson didn't throw often, and tight ends rarely ran pass routes. Diggs reluctantly honed his blocking skills when the coaches made him spend extra time on the blocking sled and in board drills. The extra practice worked, and he became a quality blocker, but he still sounds like he is begging for the football more than 20 years later.

"When you go to the tight end ... the defense had to play honest," Diggs said. "And that just opened up other opportunities for the offense."

The wide receivers needed to be excellent blockers, too, and boasted plenty of experience. Starters Tuttle and Jerry Gaillard were seniors, and backups Magwood and Jeff Stockstill were juniors.

'THUNDERFOOT' AND HIS CREW

A superb kicking game was a necessity for Ford's conservative game plan to be successful. It wouldn't have done the Tigers much good to play good defense if they didn't have a great punter to put opponents in challenging field positions or have excellent place-kickers to take advantage of every scoring opportunity.

Bob Paulling, who handled extra points and short field goals, marvels at the raw ability the Tigers' kicking specialists possessed. Punter Dale Hatcher went on to become an All-Pro in 1985 as an NFL rookie with the Los Angeles Rams and was known as "Thunderfoot" to his teammates. Donald Igwebuike, the place-kicker who came over from the soccer team, made 10-of-17 field-goal attempts during the championship season.

"There's not many around that could kick the ball like Donald could and punt the ball like Hatcher could," Paulling said. "It is pretty freakish, actually."

Paulling made up half of the unusual place-kicking combination with Igwebuike. Paulling handled kickoffs in 1979 and redshirted in 1980 behind Nigerian Obed Ariri, another soccer player turned place-kicker. After Ariri's senior season in 1980, Paulling thought he was the heir apparent to the kicking job in 1981. Then Ford brought in Igwebuike, also a Nigerian, to compete for the job. Paulling's leg wasn't as strong as Igwebuike's, but his accuracy was superb. He set the school record for consecutive extra points when he made his 36th in a row late in the 1981 season.

Paulling said the two-kicker system evolved after the second game of the 1981 season, when Clemson played Tulane at the Superdome.

Igwebuike was late for the bus leaving the team hotel, and Ford had no tolerance for the tardy. The bus left him behind, and he pulled a muscle chasing after the bus. When Igwebuike got to the Superdome, kicking was out of the question. Paulling made an extra point and two field goals that day, and Ford began using both players, though there didn't seem to be any set plan for the rotation.

"Coach Ford never predetermined who was going to kick," Paulling said. "When it was third down and he was ready to go to fourth down, we were told to go stand by Coach Ford, and he'd stick one of us in. I guess he did that on purpose to keep us both on our toes and keep the competitiveness between us."

It worked, as they combined to make 14-of-23 attempts. Paulling said they got along fine, much like the running backs who graciously shared playing time and carries. Though Paulling might have wanted to be out on the field, he pulled for Igwebuike to make kicks because he wanted to win. Their competitions during practice were breathtaking at times.

One day at the end of practice, a fierce wind was blowing off Lake Hartwell at the backs of the kickers as they practiced in live, 11-on-11 drills. Taking turns, Paulling and Igwebuike both kicked 60-yard field goals. They backed up and kicked from 66 yards. Both kicks were good. At 72 yards, Paulling finally missed, but Igwebuike made another kick. Paulling said Igwebuike made one more kick, from 78 yards, before the end of the drill.

Though he possessed great natural kicking talent, Igwebuike needed tutoring because he was unfamiliar with place-kicking after coming over from the soccer team. Paulling noticed that Igwebuike didn't seem to be crushing the ball on kickoffs nearly as hard or as far as he was capable. The kickoffs would land right around the goal line, and Paulling knew Igwebuike could kick it farther.

In Igwebuike's more familiar sport, soccer, the opponent is awarded a goal kick when the ball is knocked over the goal line. Paulling figured out that Igwebuike mistakenly thought he wasn't supposed to kick the ball over the goal line. Paulling explained to Igwebuike that it was okay to send kickoffs through the end zone.

"Then he started kicking it up on the hill [beyond the end zone] on the kickoffs," Paulling said.

SPECIAL TEAMS, SPECIAL TIMES

Ford half-jokingly took credit for Clemson's kicking game as long as it was successful, but Paulling said Ford didn't know much about kicking. George Dostal, the strength coach, worked with the kickers and punters on fundamentals and mechanics.

"It's just like hitting a golf ball," Paulling said. "You have to hit it the same every time. You have to take the same number of steps, your plant foot is very important, and the snapper and the holder are most important."

Practices were long for the kickers and punters because they started special teams work at the beginning of practice and finished at the end of practice. While the offense and defense practiced, the kickers and punters did little aside from goofing around.

They played a game called "kick back," during which players would stand on opposite sides of the field and boom kicks toward one another. They would place 55-gallon barrels around the perimeter of the field and play "punt golf," attempting to loft punts into the barrels. They did a lot of passing and catching to pass the time until they had to work with the rest of the team again at the end of practice.

The kicking work with the entire team at the end of practice took a long time, too, because Ford was adamant about allowing backup kickers and punters to work during practice. He was a champion of the underdog, known for platooning players at many positions and giving second- and third-team players opportunities they might not get on other teams.

Ford was a stickler for precision and fast-operation time, to the point where he stood with a stopwatch himself and monitored the "get-off time" for the punts and place-kicks.

"We always used to laugh about that," said holder Anthony Parete. "Ford was this old, grizzled, kind of a rough-and-tumble guy—and he's timing the kickers. It just struck us funny a little bit."

Ford's constant drilling of the kicking game and attention to detail resulted in one of the smoothest kicking operations in the nation. Parete dropped one snap on a field-goal attempt in the Tulane game, but can't remember a bad snap on a place-kick by Williams the whole season.

"It was incredible," Parete said. "The ball was just there, and all I did was change the direction of the ball. It was always put over the tee. All I did was knock it down and grab one of the points."

When the place-kickers were working, Ford would station himself 10 yards ahead of the line of scrimmage and 10 yards to the left of the formation. He would squat down with his back to the kickers and watch the balls sail through the uprights. On one occasion, a walk-on hit a kick completely wrong. The ball hooked off to the left and hit Ford square in the back.

"He had a few choice words to say about that one," Paulling said.

With the way the Clemson kickers and punters usually performed, Ford rarely had much reason to complain. Hatcher averaged 43.1 yards on 40 punts, an ACC-best. Paulling and Igwebuike combined for a reliable field-goal team, and the defense-first plan worked nearly to perfection.

ONE OF THE BEST EVER?

Academic advisor Joe White's job during practice was to supervise the kickers and punters while the offense and defense worked elsewhere.

White's experience in that area was minimal, so he never attempted to teach them mechanics. His job was to make sure they performed the drills they had been instructed to do because they were outside the view of the head coach. He made sure the kickers worked from the middle of the field and both hash marks, and he supervised some of their conditioning drills.

One of his favorite jobs was to hold the watch and measure freshman punter Dale Hatcher's hang time. Hatcher was a punting prodigy—he appeared in the national semifinals of the Punt, Pass, &

Dale Hatcher's teammates called him "Thunderfoot," and some believe he was one of the best college punters ever.

Kick contest in 1975 and 1976 and averaged 48.8 yards per punt in 1980 as a high school senior in Cheraw, South Carolina. White would look at his watch in amazement after Hatcher's punts finally crashed to earth. Later, he would report to the rest of the coaches in excited tones.

"You would not believe what I did today," White said he would tell them. "I timed Hatcher with about a 5.8 [-second] hang time on his punts."

Ray Guy, formerly of the Oakland Raiders, is almost universally recognized as the greatest punter of all time. The annual award given to the nation's best punter is named for Guy.

As a member of the Virginia Tech staff, White coached against Guy when he was punting for Southern Mississippi.

"He was a great punter," White said, "but I always thought, personally, that Dale Hatcher was the best I ever saw."

Hatcher's skills were critical to the overall construction of the team. Before four- and five-wideout sets and pass-happy offenses turned football into a high-scoring game of "basketball on grass," a generation of college coaches believed strongly in the principle of playing for field position.

If the offense didn't turn over the ball, there was value in preserving your right to punt, especially when "Thunderfoot" was doing the punting. The opponent's punter was never as good, and Clemson's defense was outstanding, so the Tigers often got the ball back in better field position than they'd had when they decided to punt.

Ripped straight from Bear Bryant's playbook, the strategy was perfect for a team Ford carefully groomed for success.

7

MODEST BEGINNINGS:
Tigers Start Slow

" Here's the defending national champion. They come with Herschel Walker, Buck Belue, the whole cast of characters that basically they won the national championship with the year before. And we beat them. **"**

—Defensive end Bill Smith

C lemson didn't impress anybody as a national championship-caliber team in its opener—least of all its legendary former coach, Frank Howard.

Wofford, a Division I-AA opponent, rushed for 165 yards and passed for 128. The Terriers scored the game's first points on Don Hairston's 24-yard field goal. Though the Tigers won 45-10, Howard wondered aloud whether the Clemson defense would be able to stop any halfway-decent opponent because some misdirection plays gave the Tigers fits.

Howard, the late legendary coach who was a veteran of 30 seasons at Clemson and won six ACC titles, was recruited as an ally by Danny

Ford. By the time Ford replaced Charley Pell as head coach at the end of the 1978 regular season, Howard had been out of coaching for nine years and didn't pose any threat to Ford's job security. Ford recognized Howard as a resource and went out of his way to welcome him to the team.

Howard had Memorial Stadium built and created the Clemson traditions of rubbing Howard's Rock and running down the hill to enter the stadium. Bringing Howard closer to the program again gained Ford support from older alumni who recognized Howard as a living, breathing icon.

"Coach Ford would go pick up Coach Howard, take him to the office, take him to functions," said wide receivers coach Lawson Holland. "Coach Howard went to a lot of our staff get-togethers, was up and down the hall in the office, loved to come in the office and draw up some plays for us. His staying involved and Coach Ford keeping him involved was a very smart move. Even though the players on Coach Ford's team never had a chance to play for Coach Howard, I think they felt his presence."

Tailback Chuck McSwain said Ford often asked Howard to speak to the team. McSwain remembers Howard's deep, gruff voice referring to the players as, "Hey, boys," and giving grandfatherly advice.

"That's one guy I would love to play for," McSwain said. "He's got that personality that you just can't help but love him. He was a nice guy, just the way he talked and carried on."

Neither Howard nor Ford nor any other coach could have had much good to say about Clemson's first-half performance against Wofford. The players say they can't repeat what Ford told them in the locker room at halftime because it's not fit for publication. They do say Ford had little tolerance for poor performances against clearly inferior opponents.

"Coach Ford always told us to win the games you're supposed to win," said wide receiver Frank Magwood.

Clemson wasn't even supposed to play Wofford that season, but it called on the Terriers in the spring of 1981 when Villanova dropped football and sent the Tigers scrambling to find an opponent. Wofford didn't just come to Memorial Stadium and roll over.

Running the wing-T under coach Buddy Sasser, the Terriers drove 73 yards to the Clemson 7-yard line on the game's opening drive before Hairston's field goal.

After a 38-yard kickoff return by Perry Tuttle, the Tigers managed just one first down on their first drive and only scored when Donald Igwebuike booted a 52-yard field goal through the uprights. Clemson's second and third drives resulted in punts.

"We didn't make anything happen offensively," said offensive coordinator Nelson Stokley. "They were giving us a little trouble on defense with some of the things they were doing."

After the game, Ford said Wofford had the best game plan of any team he had faced while at Clemson. The Tigers had abundant speed on defense, and Wofford used Clemson's aggressive pursuit to its advantage with misdirection plays.

Ford also was concerned that Clemson was heavy-legged because the weather had been unusually cool during preseason practice, so the Tigers hadn't had to work in the heat. In a way, Ford was glad the temperature was 83 degrees and the humidity was high at 69 percent, because it demonstrated that Clemson needed to work harder to get into shape—and that freshman nose guard William Perry needed to drop 10 pounds to 285 to be more effective.

Clemson did have superior depth and wore down the Terriers, rushing for 285 yards on 54 carries and setting the tone for the way the offense would run the rest of the season.

"We were going to keep pounding them and pounding them," said offensive line coach Larry Van Der Heyden. "We wanted to wear you down. That's why we tried to be really physical in practice. That's why we coached them hard. In the fourth quarter, we wanted to come on strong."

The Tigers led 17-3 by halftime thanks to Homer Jordan's 14-yard scoring run and 80-yard pass to Perry Tuttle. Wofford didn't score its touchdown until 4:36 remained in the game. By then, Jordan had passed for two touchdowns and run for two more. William Devane made three tackles behind the line of scrimmage, and Clemson won 45-10—though it did nothing to suggest it should be in the Top 25, let alone a national title contender.

"The early games it may appear that we were struggling," Holland said, "but one thing we were doing was winning. We never felt, as a staff, that we had any easy games to play; and fortunately, we kept getting better and better."

BIG 'D' IN THE BIG EASY

It would have been tempting for Clemson's players to sneak out of their hotel rooms the night before they met Tulane in New Orleans.

The revelry of Bourbon Street beckoned. But if anybody fell prey to the temptation, they're not admitting it—even more than 20 years afterward. They remembered a Gator Bowl trip from a few years earlier, when a player sneaked out after curfew.

"Coach Ford put him on the bus and sent him home," said center Tony Berryhill. "We knew you needed to stay in your own place."

The atmosphere at the Superdome provided enough of a thrill for Clemson's players. Though the Tigers played in a stadium that was plenty big, the vast expanse of this indoor facility was awe-inspiring.

"It was all business," said defensive tackle Ray Brown. "We stayed right there at the Hyatt, which was connected to the Superdome. We were just all small-town players. ... The Superdome in itself was a party for us. Playing on Astroturf was a new thing, too."

The fans honored the Clemson tradition of bringing two-dollar bills stamped with Tiger paws to demonstrate the amount of money Clemson followers could add to a local economy when they followed their team.

Though the fans enjoyed Bourbon Street, the players were focused on winning the game and were amazed enough at the Superdome. It wasn't much bigger than Death Valley in terms of capacity, but the fact that so many seats were in an indoor arena was incredible.

"We were all like Hoosiers going to the state championship walking in that big stadium," said defensive tackle Dan Benish. "Even though we played at Clemson in front of a lot of people, that game showed a lot about our character, who we were and who our fans were."

During a walk-through on the day before the game, Dale Hatcher explored the space with his punting, hitting the gondola that held the scoreboard 155 feet overhead. The only players who had done that before were Ray Guy, the great Oakland Raiders punter, and Russell Erxleben, the strong-legged New England Patriots punter.

"That was a big deal," said place-kicker Bob Paulling. "Hatcher went in there and he hit it about eight times in a row, one right after the other. The people with the Superdome went in there and made him quit. They said he was going to tear the thing up if he didn't quit."

Berryhill didn't have the greatest visit to Tulane, though he's not sure what brought about his problems. It might have been that Clemson was playing Tulane at night rather than in the afternoon, and Berryhill's eating schedule was thrown off. Berryhill ate breakfast but didn't have much lunch, and that's never good for an offensive lineman. In the middle of the afternoon, Berryhill and some other players were hungry. They ordered room service. It's possible Berryhill ate something that made him sick. It's possible he just ate too much, too close to kickoff. Whatever the case, he was in bad shape on the field. He was vomiting, and he couldn't stop, but he didn't let his ailment hinder his play. He used the gross-out factor to his advantage.

Certain blocks are easier for an offensive lineman if his defender is lined up in a certain position. Berryhill used his vomiting to put his defenders in position to be blocked. If Berryhill needed the nose guard to be on his right, he threw up to the left. The nose guard would scuttle away from Berryhill's stomach contents and give Berryhill a perfect blocking angle.

That was a good thing, because the Tigers needed every advantage they could get as they gained just 177 yards of offense in a 13-5 victory.

For the second-straight game against an inferior opponent, Clemson started slowly. Tulane led 5-0 after getting a 46-yard field goal from Vince Manalla and a safety when Hatcher fell on an errant snap in the end zone. The Tiger defense got things started when William Devane forced a Tulane fumble and Joe Glenn recovered at the Tulane 25. Five plays later, Cliff Austin ran four yards over center to score the game's only touchdown.

Paulling added field goals of 31 and 37 yards in the fourth quarter, and the defense that had so concerned Frank Howard came up big, shutting out the Green Wave over the final three quarters. Clemson recovered three fumbles and intercepted four passes, foreshadowing the festival of turnovers that would follow in its next game—at home against Georgia.

The Tigers held Tulane to 40 rushing yards, 177 yards of total offense, and five first downs. Glenn had two of Clemson's four sacks plus the fumble recovery. Clemson won by eight in a game Benish said isn't often appreciated because of the narrow margin. Benish considers the victory one of the more impressive performances by Clemson in his career because the Tigers won in a strange environment.

"I think it was a big game that people don't talk about, and I think it was a big game in our minds," said defensive tackle Dan Benish.

PAYBACK TIME VS. BULLDOGS

One remarkable quarter for Scott Woerner created a whole year of angst for Clemson's players. In 1980, Woerner returned a punt 67 yards for the game's first touchdown in Athens. Then he returned an interception 97 yards to set up a 1-yard touchdown run by Buck Belue. Georgia scored the game's first 14 points and won 20-16 on the way to a 12-0 record and the national title.

Clemson's defense was nearly impenetrable in that game. The Tigers held the national champions to 157 yards, though Herschel Walker rushed for 121 on 23 carries. Clemson gained 351 yards but couldn't overcome the Bulldogs' early lead.

"We should have won that game," Benish said.

Though the Tigers finished a disappointing 6-5 in 1980, the close call against the national champion gave them confidence that they could play with anybody—a narrow defeat that gave them a revenge factor heading into the 1981 rematch.

The team already was fired up when Ford entered the locker room before the kickoff. Jerry Gaillard said Ford delivered an unforgettable pregame speech about Georgia coach Vince Dooley.

"I could go out on the 50-yard line and whip Vince Dooley's [butt]," Gaillard remembered Ford saying. "I know I can. And I'd do it out there in front of thousands of people. So what you've got to do is go out there and whip the man's [butt] right in front of you."

Linebacker Danny Triplett set the tone early in the game. Wide receiver Perry Tuttle remembers seeing a flag on the field and wondering what the infraction was. Then he saw Triplett in the middle of the Georgia huddle, face to face with Walker. A country boy from Boone, North Carolina, Triplett was known for throwing his body around without any concern for his own safety. He didn't back down from anybody.

"Every single time you touch the ball, we're going to kick your [butt]," Triplett told Walker.

WALKER A WONDER

Walker was perhaps the most feared back in college football. A sophomore, Walker was fast, physical, and the target of the Clemson defense from the moment he stepped onto the field.

"If you let him get started he would kill you," said defensive tackle William Devane.

Nobody on Clemson's team knew Walker better than tight end Bubba Diggs. Growing up in Augusta, Georgia, Diggs was familiar with Walker, who went to high school 75 miles away in Wrightsville, Georgia.

Diggs saw Walker play many times in high school, when he ran over and around helpless, hapless competitors and became a national curiosity, rushing for 6,317 yards and 86 touchdowns in his career. Diggs saw Walker sprint in the Georgia Relays and was amazed with his speed and strength and with the modesty of Walker's family members.

Diggs remembers watching Wrightsville play in the state finals— along with virtually every high school coach in the nation—as defenders grasped helplessly at Walker.

"Who can tackle him?" Diggs said. "I'm being serious. The only time they had a chance was to gang tackle him. One man could not tackle him."

Walker visited Clemson the weekend the Tigers played host to Georgia and won 12-7 in 1979. Running backs coach Chuck Reedy said Walker came to three of Clemson's first four home games that year.

One of the most heated recruiting battles ever in the South appeared to be won by Clemson at one point.

"After the [1979 Georgia] game, Herschel told us he was coming to Clemson," Reedy said. "He got all wrapped up in that thing."

The commitment obviously didn't hold up. Diggs was Walker's player host when he made his official visit to Clemson and counseled his teammates the first time they played Walker in 1980 that the freshman was for real. He told the outside linebackers that they'd better not get caught inside when Walker got outside, because they wouldn't catch him if they did.

In 1981, Walker never got started as the Tigers applied fierce pressure up front. They gang tackled him, making him pay for the 111 yards he gained on 28 carries. He didn't score a touchdown against the Tigers, who had the distinction of holding Walker, the 1982 Heisman Trophy winner—and South Carolina Heisman winner George Rogers—without touchdowns in their memorable careers.

Linebackers Triplett and Jeff Davis made 11 tackles apiece. Teammates remember Davis playing like a man possessed, making 11 tackles.

"I was looking for Herschel the first half," is Davis' famous quote from that game. "He was looking for me the second half."

'WE WERE IN THEIR FACE'

Caught in the crossfire was unfortunate Georgia quarterback Buck Belue. Walker wasn't gaining enough rushing yards to make the play-action game effective, so the fake handoffs to Walker didn't slow the pass rush much. Belue had to throw with Clemson defensive linemen and linebackers constantly in his face.

Defensive tackle Dan Benish pressures Georgia quarterback Buck Belue, who threw five interceptions in Clemson's 13-3 victory.

"He was a good quarterback, don't get me wrong," said strong safety Tim Childers. "I just don't think he could see what he was doing."

Georgia appeared ready to score first with a first-and-10 on the Tigers' 17 in the first quarter. The Clemson defense held when Jeff Suttle recovered a Walker fumble. Clemson was sloppy, too, on offense, as quarterback Homer Jordan and wide receiver Frank Magwood both fumbled in Georgia territory.

Belue's second interception in a three-minute period finally led to the game's only touchdown. Childers returned four yards to the Bulldogs' 18, and four plays later, Jordan hit Perry Tuttle for eight yards and a touchdown.

Another Walker fumble with 29 seconds left in the second quarter made a huge difference in the momentum heading into halftime. Instead of going into the locker room behind just 7-0 despite four first-half turnovers, the Bulldogs watched Donald Igwebuike kick a 39-yard field goal with 11 seconds remaining in the half. At the intermission, Georgia had five turnovers and trailed 10-0.

"A lot of the credit, 80 percent of it, goes to the pressure that was applied to Buck Belue and the line of scrimmage," Childers said. "I know Buck Belue didn't have time to look for one receiver at the most."

Walker's best opportunity to make a big play came when he got to the perimeter on the first possession of the third quarter. One player, cornerback Anthony Rose, stood between Walker and a possible touchdown. Rose still remembers how the tackling fundamentals drilled into his head for years started racing through his mind.

Rose wanted to protect the corner, because he knew if Walker got around the end he would score. Rose used the sideline to get Walker to cut back to the middle, then floored him with a textbook tackle.

"I was in perfect position," Rose said. "I just put my head to the side, came out of my stance, drove through, and brought him down."

Walker gained 21 yards, and the Bulldogs had to settle for a 40-yard field goal from Kevin Butler to cut the deficit to 10-3.

Igwebuike answered with a 29-yard field goal in the first minute of the fourth quarter, and Clemson's defense wasn't about to squander a 10-point lead. Billy Davis, Rose, and Rod McSwain all intercepted Belue passes. Two interceptions came on consecutive attempts, and Clemson won 13-3.

"When they tried to throw the ball, we were in their face," said defensive tackle Dan Benish. "When they tried to run the ball, we were all over them."

Georgia had been ranked No. 4 in the nation entering the game, and Clemson had never defeated an opponent ranked that high. The victory and a 3-0 record got the Tigers attention from the pollsters, and they debuted at No. 19 according to The Associated Press and No. 18 by the United Press International.

Winning also built confidence among the players that this could be a special season.

"It was like, 'Okay, we beat last year's national champ, and if we stick to our mission, everything will fall into place,'" said defensive tackle Ray Brown. "And we did. If we just do like they did [in 1980] and don't lose anything, they can't take it from us."

Belue now hosts a talk radio show in Atlanta. Clemson is often the butt of jokes among callers to the show in an audience dominated by Georgia Bulldog fans. Benish listens to the show and said Belue usually puts in a good word for Clemson when others make fun of the Tigers.

More than 20 years after the game, Benish wound up coaching Belue's nephew. Lance Belue quarterbacked the team of 10-year-olds and is proud of his uncle's football history.

Benish couldn't resist giving Belue grief through Lance about the 1981 game.

"You can tell your Uncle Buck not to come around here," Benish told Lance, "because he's got nothing on us."

Diggs spoke briefly to Walker on the field after the 1981 game, but Walker couldn't stick around long because his security detail whisked him away to the locker room. Their next memorable meeting came on May 29, 1983, in a game in the now-defunct United States Football League.

The Washington Generals awarded Diggs the special teams player of the game award that day because he made two tackles on Walker, who was playing for the New Jersey Generals. One tackle was pure luck, as Diggs was hoping and praying Walker wouldn't run over him. After that game, Walker told Diggs he didn't realize Diggs could play defense.

"I told him I didn't know I could tackle Herschel Walker," Diggs said.

KENTUCKY: LESSON IN FAITH

Joe White, the Clemson team academic advisor who helped coach kickers and punters, was livid as the teams went to the locker room on October 3 at Kentucky for halftime.

Early in the second quarter, Clemson had the ball near the Kentucky goal line after Jeff Bryant recovered a fumble at the 16-yard line. On third-and-goal from the 1-yard line, Cliff Austin leaped over left tackle for no gain. Clemson called timeout and decided to go for the touchdown on fourth down.

As Austin ran off left guard, White watched the official on the Clemson sideline. The official started to raise his arms to signal a Tiger touchdown, then dropped his arms back to his side.

From the other sideline, another official came running along the goal line to mark the ball. The ball was placed a few inches short of the goal line and awarded to Kentucky. When the half was over, White confronted the official who obviously had changed his mind during the course of the play.

White and Clemson learned the horror of working with a split officiating crew. Some of the officials were from the ACC, some from the SEC. On the play at the goal line, the ACC ref was the one who ran in from the other side to mark the ball.

The official who almost raised his arms was from the SEC.

"He said, 'Well, it's your guy's call, and your guy didn't call it,'" White said.

After his fruitless protest, White went to the locker room despondent. He sat down in a corner, lowered his head, and shook it over and over again. White and the entire Clemson coaching staff had reason to be upset.

A week after dethroning defending-national champion Georgia at Clemson, the Tigers trailed an inferior opponent at Kentucky. The only score of the first half was a 40-yard field goal by Tom Griggs.

Clemson's defense had played well, holding Kentucky to 120 yards on 39 plays; but the Tigers had been anemic on offense. Their longest play in the first half was nine yards. Homer Jordan was 1-for-6 passing for eight yards, and Clemson had 65 yards of total offense.

"We had so many opportunities and didn't take advantage," White said.

Tight end Bubba Diggs finally got the Tigers going in the second half. On the second play from scrimmage of the third quarter, Diggs caught a 24-yard pass from Jordan. Diggs hadn't caught a pass all season, but this was to be Clemson's longest reception of the day at a moment when the Tigers needed a big play.

Diggs admitted that he went a little nuts after making the catch.

"I caught my first pass of the year," Diggs said. "Perry Tuttle laughed at me. He said I was acting like a kid on a doggone rollercoaster ride. But I was so excited. We didn't throw the ball to the tight ends or whatever, and I kept a drive alive."

Diggs made the most of an opportunity he felt didn't happen often enough. He grew up believing his strengths were running pass routes and catching the ball. He was greatly frustrated to arrive at Clemson and find that tight ends were little more than offensive tackles in Danny Ford's offense.

"There were times when I wanted to throw the hat in and say I should have gone somewhere where they threw the ball because I knew I could do one thing, which was receiving and running with the ball," Diggs said.

Jordan also completed an 18-yard pass to Frank Magwood on third-and-12 from the Kentucky 33 on that drive, and Kevin Mack scored off left tackle on third-and-6 from the 11.

The game quickly turned in Clemson's favor. Andy Headen recovered a fumble at Kentucky's 22, and Jordan ran three yards for a score and a 14-3 lead. Kentucky drove to the Clemson 14, but Danny Triplett intercepted with 8:10 remaining in the fourth quarter. Clemson clinched the game with a determined, 12-play, 94-yard drive for a touchdown. Tailback Chuck McSwain carried five times for 41 yards on the drive, scoring on a 3-yard run with 2:48 to play for the final points in a 21-3 victory.

In the second half, the Tigers held a time of possession advantage of 19:09 to 10:51. The Clemson defense held Kentucky to 97 second-half yards. Afterward in the locker room, running backs coach Chuck Reedy and offensive coordinator Nelson Stokley made fun of White for his halftime despondency.

"Boy, didn't you trust us?" they asked. "Didn't you have any faith in us?"

After it was over, Danny Ford commended his players for their poise. He told them it was time to start thinking about earning ACC championship rings, and awarded the game ball to defensive coordinator Tom Harper, the Kentucky graduate whose unit held his alma mater to a field goal.

Clemson moved into the top 10 when the polls came out, ranked No. 9 by The Associated Press and No. 10 by the United Press International. Four games into the season, the Tigers were gaining national recognition and confidence as they prepared for their ACC opener against Virginia.

8

TRADITIONAL RIVALS:
The ACC and the Gamecocks

" I'm a firm believer in confidence, and believing you're going to win is 90 percent of the battle. ... They just continued to get better and better and gained more and more confidence every week. That was a trademark of that team. They improved every week, really up to the Orange Bowl. **"**

—Running backs coach Chuck Reedy

Every great defensive football team wants to shut out an opponent, and Clemson was a great defensive team in 1981.

The Tigers didn't give up a rushing touchdown until the seventh game. They forced 41 turnovers over the course of the season and never allowed more than 24 points. Despite those accomplishments, their season wouldn't have been complete without a shutout.

"We actually had a goal before every game, and we talked about it; and that was to hold the opposing teams to no points," said Clemson cornerback Anthony Rose. "We called it a 'goose egg.'"

That Virginia was going to present one of Clemson's best opportunities to get a goose egg was no secret. The Cavaliers hadn't won more than two games in ACC play since 1973, and their only victory in 1981 came later against Division I-AA Virginia Military Institute in a 13-10 nailbiter. Virginia already had lost 3-0 at Rutgers and entered the Clemson game with an 0-4 record—but had lost its previous three games by just five points or less.

Clemson had a long history of defeating the Cavaliers, winning 20 straight games at that point. Longtime former head coach Frank Howard used to deride Virginia as "white meat" because of the way the Tigers devoured the Cavaliers.

The late Bob Bradley, the sports information director whose promotion of Clemson helped put the school on the map, used to love telling how a bespectacled, professorial-looking Virginia fan once taunted Howard in Charlottesville. Bradley said the fan told Howard that Virginia was going to get Clemson this time.

"Your granddaddy used to say the same thing," Howard supposedly replied.

Virginia's offense crossed midfield once in the first half and had a second-and-2 from the Clemson 37-yard line. But Jeff Bryant stopped a Derek Jenkins run over left guard for one yard, and Gordie Whitehead passed incomplete to bring up fourth-and-1. Rather than try to get the first down, Virginia coach Dick Bestwick elected to punt and try to keep the Tigers deep in their own end, ruining one of the Cavaliers' best scoring chances.

Thanks to Cliff Austin's 43-yard scoring burst around the right end in the second quarter, Clemson led 10-0 at halftime. The Tiger offense took control in the third quarter, grinding out touchdown drives of 11 and 14 plays and consuming all but 2:25 of the 15 minutes on the clock.

By the time Virginia threatened to score again, it was late in the fourth quarter, and the Tigers led 27-0. The Cavaliers drove to the Clemson 5-yard line for a first-and-goal, but Terry Kinard stopped Jenkins off right tackle for no gain. Jeff Suttle sacked Whitehead for a

10-yard loss, and Whitehead passed incomplete twice to turn over the ball on downs.

"Virginia was one of those games where everything fell together," Rose said. "Anytime you did that [shut out an opponent], it was pretty special."

Jeff Davis led the defense with 11 tackles; Jeff Bryant made three tackles behind the line of scrimmage; and Andy Headen broke up three passes. Clemson had its shutout, and its fans celebrated with some taunting during the first rainy home game in three years at Death Valley.

"They were chanting, 'Put Ralph in,'" said Clemson tailback Chuck McSwain.

The fans were referring, of course, to Ralph Sampson, the 7-foot-4 center for Virginia who was one of the greatest players in college basketball history. Perhaps if he were around—and they could have found football cleats to fit him—the Cavaliers could have sent Sampson out to catch a jump ball on a fade route on that one drive inside the Clemson 10-yard line.

It's more likely, though, that nothing was going to stand between this Clemson defense and a shutout on that day. The poll voters took notice, moving the Tigers to No. 6 in the AP and No. 7 in the UPI polls.

DEVILS' DUE: AUSTIN RUNS WILD

Clemson might well have overlooked Duke if the Tigers weren't so red-faced over what happened the previous season against the Blue Devils. Entering the 1980 game with Duke, Clemson was 4-1 with plenty of aspirations for an appearance in a quality bowl game. The Tigers' only loss had been by four points to Georgia, which went on to win the national championship.

All that changed against Duke. Dennis Tabron intercepted three Homer Jordan passes, returning one 87 yards for the game-clinching touchdown in a 34-17 drubbing of the Tigers at Death Valley.

The Clemson players were shocked. Duke had a quality quarterback in Ben Bennett, who threw for 257 yards that day, but nobody at Clemson imagined Duke had a chance of winning that game.

"Duke is a very successful university in itself, but moreso known for basketball," said Clemson tight end Bubba Diggs. "We didn't want to be known as the team getting beat by Duke or whatever. They didn't play football like we did. You could go to Duke and see the corners of the end zones or portions of the stands empty. Not like Death Valley—regardless of whether you win or lose, that place was going to be sold out."

Duke couldn't blame the attendance at Wallace Wade Stadium in 1981 on the weather. Though skies were clear and a gentle northerly wind was blowing with the temperature a comfortable 63 degrees, just 26,000 fans attended.

Bennett—a superb passing quarterback—again had a good day statistically with 243 passing yards as Duke managed 23 first downs. It mattered little because Clemson tailback Cliff Austin had perhaps his best game ever in a 38-10 beating.

Austin carried 19 times for 178 yards—a season high for the Tigers, who led 24-3 by halftime. Austin scored two touchdowns as he sparked Clemson to a 323-yard performance on the ground.

Terry Kinard intercepted two passes to spark the defense, and Clemson's march upward in the polls continued. The Tigers moved to fourth in the AP and UPI rankings.

ATTACKING THE PACK

There were just two teams in the ACC that Clemson hadn't defeated in the previous two seasons under Danny Ford. One was Maryland, which the Tigers would face later in the season with the ACC championship on the line. The other was N.C. State, whose demographics bore an uncanny resemblance to Clemson's.

Both are land-grant schools that have healthy agriculture programs and operate extension services for farmers and the community. Each has a healthy rivalry with a university that is a namesake in its state—N.C.

State with the University of North Carolina and Clemson with the University of South Carolina.

N.C. State also had an All-ACC tailback, Joe McIntosh, and some other players who had chosen to join the Wolfpack rather than the Tigers. Clemson's players talked before the game about showing those players they had made a mistake, but it didn't look that way early.

Cliff Austin fumbled on Clemson's first possession, and N.C. State's Rick Etheridge recovered at the Tiger 41-yard line. McIntosh carried six times for 25 yards on the ensuing N.C. State touchdown drive, and Larmount Lawson ran 13 yards off the right tackle for the opening score.

After that, the Clemson defense didn't give N.C. State anything as Jeff Davis had one of his best games. He made 19 tackles, three behind the line of scrimmage, including one sack. Jeff Bryant made 12 tackles, four of them for 1-yard losses.

On offense, Clemson surprised N.C. State with a new formation. On some plays, the Tigers used the wishbone, placing three running backs behind Jordan, something they did on occasion over the rest of the season to take advantage of their talent and depth in the backfield.

"We had never done that before," said offensive coordinator Nelson Stokley. "We basically were an I-formation team. We got into the wishbone a few times, and it really helped us. It allowed us to get good players on the field."

Nonetheless, the Clemson offense didn't have its best day. Homer Jordan attempted 14 passes and completed as many (three) to N.C. State's players as Clemson's players. Austin and Kevin Mack lost fumbles as well.

But Jordan rushed for 104 yards on 21 carries and raced against the clock to engineer a 65-yard drive that culminated in a 1-yard Austin touchdown run with 13 seconds remaining in the second quarter to give Clemson a 10-7 halftime lead.

Fullback Jeff McCall added a 15-yard touchdown run with 8:30 left in the game for the final margin in a 17-7 victory.

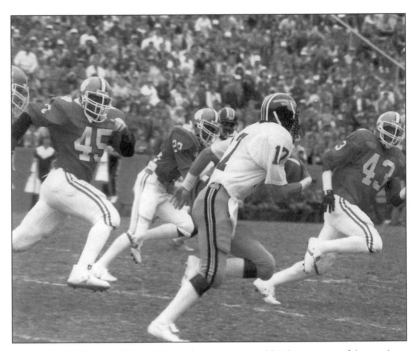

Linebacker Jeff Davis (45) and free safety Terry Kinard (43) were two of the anchors of a Clemson defense that held opponents to 8.8 points per game.

"I remember going to the right, seeing a hole and jumping over somebody and running to the end zone, dragging somebody into the end zone," McCall said.

Clemson broke new ground in the AP poll after the victory with a No. 4 ranking that was the school's highest in history. The Tigers were No. 4 in the UPI poll and headed for a statistically dominant performance the likes of which the ACC had never before witnessed.

WAKE FOREST: SCORING BINGE

Bob Paulling ran on the field for his eighth extra-point attempt of the day against Wake Forest, but felt a tug on his jersey as he prepared to kick. Lockie Brown, a senior backup kicker, was standing behind him. Brown had never kicked in a game before, and he was nervous and speechless. Paulling asked Brown if he was supposed to kick. Brown nodded. Paulling ran off the field, and Brown booted the ball through the uprights.

There are many such stories about the Wake Forest game, when Clemson set an ACC scoring record that stands to this day. The Tigers won 82-24, rushed for 536 yards and gained 756 yards of total offense.

Al Groh, the first-year Wake Forest coach who later went on to coach Virginia and the New York Jets, feared it would be a long day before the Deacons even entered the stadium.

"What do you think?" Groh remembers an assistant asking as the team got off the bus to head to the locker room.

Groh thought about the Deacons' talent, the number of players left home with injuries, and the quality of the team Wake Forest was about to face.

"I think we might have trouble ever stopping them," Groh said.

He was right. Clemson never punted, fumbled, or threw an interception. The Tigers never even kicked a field goal, scoring touchdowns on all 12 possessions. Clemson set 11 school records and tied three more, also breaking four ACC records. But the statistics aren't what the players remember about Wake Forest. They remember the game on Halloween for the amount of athletes who had an opportunity to play because it was a blowout.

The Tigers carried about 115 to 118 on their roster, and many participated only in practice because only 11 can play at one time. For the backups and walk-ons, this was the opportunity of a lifetime.

"A lot of those guys didn't have anything to do except dress out during homecoming," Paulling said. "For those fellas to actually have the opportunity to play a game during the national championship season was really special for a lot of people."

Freshman defensive end Steve Berlin hadn't played all season and was delighted that his mother, Dolores Berlin, had come from Pittsburgh to see the game. As the deficit grew, he realized that he was going to have a chance to play for the first time in a Clemson uniform.

Wake Forest quarterback Gary Schofield dropped back to pass on Berlin's first play as a Tiger in the middle of the fourth quarter. Berlin shot through a gap between guard and tackle and made a sack on his first snap.

"I jumped up, and I was so happy and my mom was there," Berlin said. "That was pretty special."

Eleven Clemson players had rushing yardage, and nine players scored. The most memorable play might have been the second carry of freshman Craig Crawford's career. Crawford—who initially didn't even dress for the game—ran 72 yards for a touchdown and what was the 10th-longest run from scrimmage in school history. Duke Holloman, who carried 11 times all season, also scored a touchdown on a 3-yard run.

"We pulled guys out of the stands and told them to go get dressed so they could play," said defensive end Ray Brown. "It was giving the guys an opportunity to play in front of their parents for the first time, and the chance to play in front of that big a crowd for the first time in their whole life."

At No. 2 in the AP and No. 3 in the UPI polls, the Tigers were getting close to the coveted No. 1 ranking.

BRYANT MAKES HEELS BLUE

For as long as anyone can remember, a mutual disrespect has existed between Clemson and North Carolina.

Stereotypically, North Carolina students, alumni, and fans have looked down on Clemson because of its agrarian roots and because North Carolina usually is ranked among the top few public universities in the nation.

Clemson folks despise North Carolina because they perceive snootiness and because they believe North Carolina's location near the center of the ACC's power base in Greensboro gets the Tar Heels favors from the conference.

Once a Tar Heel, always a Tar Heel, Clemson fans say.

"It's a beautiful school," said Clemson defensive tackle Dan Benish. "I liked it. It's a great place to go up and play, but the people around you just make you feel like they are superior to you."

When Benish played in the NFL, he became friendly with former North Carolina defensive end Donnell Thompson. They worked out with each other and talked about the hatred fans of the two schools had for one another. Benish traced his own bitterness toward North Carolina to the game in 1980 at Clemson.

"We hated each other," Benish said. "They hated Clemson, and we hated them."

Clemson trailed by five and had first-and-goal at the North Carolina 1-yard line on its final possession. After two Clemson running plays both resulted in no gain, Lawrence Taylor sacked Homer Jordan for a 9-yard loss on third down. A Jordan pass for Jerry Gaillard with 21 seconds remaining fell incomplete, and the Tar Heels held on to win 24-19. Taylor made two sacks, both on critical drives in the fourth quarter. Jordan remembers reading a book written by Taylor years later and finding he was in it because he was the victim of one of the biggest sacks of Taylor's college career.

"He grabbed me by my collar, and it seemed like he was twirling me around like a little towel," Jordan said.

The history of ill will toward each other, the resentment from the previous year, and the fact that this was the first time top-10 ranked teams met in an ACC game had emotions running high.

Clemson's players came running onto the field and were jumping around and smacking one another on the helmets in anticipation of the biggest game in ACC history. Punt returner Billy Davis looked over at defensive coordinator Tom Harper on the sideline.

"He is sitting on the bench, one arm back, leaning back and smoking a cigarette," Davis said. "He was either taking it all in or gathering himself. Everybody else was jumping around like maniacs, and Coach Harper was just sitting there, smoking a cigarette, surveying the scene."

Harper might have been calm because he knew his defense was going to play well even as the sides sniped viciously at one another. Several Clemson players said they can't ever remember more trash talk or cheap shots in a game.

Benish said he watched with disbelief as Kelvin Bryant, North Carolina's skinny but talented tailback, mouthed off at him.

"I'm looking at him," Benish said. "I'm like, 'Are you serious? You're half my size.' It was that kind of stuff, that kind of banter going back and forth."

Benish sprained his knee in that game, and Clemson fullback Jeff McCall suffered two broken ribs when an opponent speared him from behind. McCall had 16 carries for a season-high 84 yards and the game's only touchdown.

"That's all we want to do," McCall remembered the tackler saying after spearing him. "We wanted to get you out of here."

Clemson's defense saved the day. Twice North Carolina drove inside the Clemson 10-yard line only to settle for field goals by Brooks Barwick. The Tigers held North Carolina to 84 rushing yards and forced quarterback Scott Stankavage to misfire on 12 of his 21 passing attempts. Benish, Jeff Bryant, and William Perry each made two tackles behind the line of scrimmage and one quarterback sack. The defense didn't give up a touchdown, as the Tar Heels' scoring came on two field goals and a safety when Danny Barlow blocked Dale Hatcher's punt through the end zone.

The Tar Heels were driving toward a possible game-winning field goal when Clemson defensive tackle Jeff Bryant made perhaps the most important play of the entire season.

On first-and-10 from the North Carolina 40, the Tar Heels set up a screen pass to Alan Burrus. Stankavage passed out to his right, but Burrus couldn't make the catch. Bill Smith, Clemson's left defensive end, tackled Burrus and thought the play was over.

"The ball was right in front of me," Smith said. "I was there laying on top of the guy that was supposed to catch the pass, and the next thing you know, Jeff Bryant falls on the ball, and everybody else is like, 'It's an incomplete pass.'

"It was a lateral, but nobody knew that except Jeff, I guess."

The only important thing was that Bryant and the game officials saw the play the same way. Fifty-seven seconds remained, and Clemson had held on to win 10-8.

The Tigers celebrated with the same song after every victory, with the exception of South Carolina, when they sang the "Cockadoodledoo Song." The feeling of accomplishment was especially acute this time as they sang: "We don't give a [darn] about the whole state of North Carolina, the whole state of North Carolina, the whole state of North Carolina. We don't give a [darn] about the whole state of North Carolina. We're from Clemson U."

Clemson U. had just won the most highly anticipated game in ACC history. The Tigers were No. 2 in both polls after winning. They needed one more victory to clinch the ACC title and had another of their biggest rivals standing in the way.

MARYLAND: ACC TITLE ON THE LINE

The players on the 1981 team often say they had an excellent passing attack but seldom used it because coach Danny Ford preferred to punish opposing defenses with the running game. Clemson proved those claims against Maryland in the victory that clinched the ACC title. The Terrapins had been ACC runners-up in each of the last three seasons. They entered the game with a 3-1 conference record and could have claimed the ACC championship by defeating Clemson and then Virginia the following week.

Maryland had stuffed Ford's ground-based attack in each of the previous two seasons, winning 19-0 in 1979 at Clemson and 34-7 in 1980 at College Park, Maryland. Clemson wide receiver Jerry Gaillard said the Terrapins succeeded by using an extra defensive end instead of a safety, playing an eight-man front and outmuscling the Tigers.

Gaillard said the wide receivers often were called upon to block that extra defensive end, and it frankly was more than they could handle.

"You pay for the size difference," Gaillard said. "They can literally just take you and throw you around like a rag doll."

If Maryland was bigger, though, that meant the Tigers were faster. Clemson exploited that advantage in the passing game after considerable hand-wringing on the part of the coaching staff heading into the game.

The assistant coaches on offense met with coordinator Nelson Stokley from Sunday night through Monday morning and decided they would have to throw a lot to beat the Terrapins' eight-man front. They presented their idea to Ford, who told them Clemson was a running team, and they had better huddle again and come up with a new plan.

"We're not doing anything else," Stokley said the assistants responded. "This is what we're going to do."

The assistants met again, late Monday night and into Tuesday morning and were more convinced than ever that throwing the ball gave them the best chance to win. They approached Ford again Tuesday evening. Again, Ford told them to forget it.

Finally, on Wednesday, Ford caved in. He told the assistants, and Stokley in particular, that they would be responsible for talking to the media after the game after Clemson lost because it veered from its usual game plan. They were to explain to reporters that throwing the ball wasn't Ford's idea.

"That was Coach Ford's way of challenging," said wide receivers coach Lawson Holland. "I think he knew that was the way we would get our best effort, even though it was going away from what we had done to be successful."

The Terrapins had a left-handed sophomore quarterback named Boomer Esiason, who would go on to fame with the Cincinnati Bengals and later in the broadcast booth. Clemson had Homer Jordan, who had more rushing attempts than pass completions that season.

Guess who had the big day as a passer? Jordan passed for 270 yards, then the third-highest total in school history, and threw for three touchdowns. He started slowly, as a pass intended for Perry Tuttle was intercepted by Howard Eubanks on Clemson's first drive. Late in the first quarter, though, Jordan skillfully engineered a scoring drive.

The Tigers took possession after a punt on their own 39-yard line with 1:53 remaining in the second quarter. Jordan completed all four of his passes on the drive—the first three for first downs and the last to Tuttle for 14 yards and a touchdown with four seconds remaining for a 7-0 halftime lead.

Jerry Gaillard made the only touchdown catch of his career in his final home game as a senior against Maryland.

Jordan and Tuttle connected again for five yards and a touchdown on the Tigers' opening drive of the second quarter. On the next drive, Clemson didn't even bother attempting a run. Jordan passed 30 yards to Tuttle and 13 yards to Frank Magwood for a first-and-10 from the 12. That set up one of the most memorable moments of Gaillard's life.

Throughout his career, Gaillard played the supporting actor to Tuttle's lead in the wide receiving corps. Tuttle was the flashy wideout with the great speed to catch deep balls and an electric personality. Gaillard was the hard-working, tough-blocking possession receiver. They were compared to the duo of spectacular Jerry Butler and steady Dwight Clark from the teams of the 1970s, though Gaillard didn't go on to make it big in the pros like Clark. Gaillard didn't have a touchdown catch entering the final home game of his senior year. With the ball on the 12, Jordan looked at Gaillard in the huddle.

"This is coming to you, Jerry," he said.

As Gaillard came open on a fade route, Jordan lofted a pass. Gaillard caught it in the end zone, and Clemson led 21-0 with two minutes left in the half.

Tuttle still had a big day, making 10 receptions to fall just one shy of the school record with 151 receiving yards and two touchdowns. Gaillard had his moment, though, and no one could take it away. He still has the game ball in his basement.

Esiason's day wasn't as memorable.

Clemson linebacker Jeff Davis entered the game with something to prove because Maryland tailback Charlie Wysocki had knocked him out the previous year when Davis was making a tackle. Wysocki's knee hit the back of Davis' head, leaving him woozy with a concussion.

When Fred Hoover, the team athletic trainer, came onto to the field, Davis was obstinate. He wanted to stay in the game. Davis doesn't curse, but said teammates have told him he was swearing during that game.

They told him all he said afterward, over and over, was that he couldn't believe the Tigers had lost 34-7. Everybody on the defense wanted to erase the memories of the 34 points the Terrapins scored the year before.

Rod McSwain blocked a punt that was recovered by Johnny Rembert for Clemson's first touchdown in the regular season finale against rival South Carolina.

"You don't say revenge," said defensive tackle William Devane. "You don't say payback. But the previous game the year before, we had it in our mind that we did take a thumping."

This time, Davis did most of the thumping, making 16 tackles. Wysocki, who rushed for 106 yards in the 1980 game, was held to 59. Joe Glenn sacked Esiason twice as Clemson recorded five sacks. Twenty-three of Esiason's 38 passes fell incomplete, and he passed for just 167 yards.

Afterward, Stokley playfully reminded Ford who was the architect of the game plan that worked so well, but that didn't matter much to anybody.

With their conference title secure and a 10-0 record, the Tigers headed into their regular-season finale with rival South Carolina ranked No. 2 in the nation.

CHICKEN HUNTING IN COLUMBIA

Things went downhill for South Carolina after Clemson's 27-6 victory in 1980 saved Danny Ford's job and launched the Tigers into the marvelous 1981 season.

The Gamecocks went on to the Gator Bowl, where they lost 37-9 to Pittsburgh. Heisman Trophy winner George Rogers was a senior on that team, and it quickly became obvious in 1981 how much South Carolina had depended on him.

South Carolina entered the Clemson game in 1981 with a 6-4 record. The Tigers had much more at risk with an undefeated season and a shot at a national title on the line, but South Carolina got off to the quick start in Columbia. Johnnie Wright's 1-yard touchdown run up the middle capped the Gamecocks' opening drive, forcing Clemson to punt on each of the first two drives. Clemson's defense held on the Gamecocks' second possession, though, and Rod McSwain got one of the most memorable days for his family off to a good start by blocking Chris Norman's punt. McSwain came from the outside and blocked the punt cleanly, and Johnny Rembert fell on the ball in the end zone.

Oranges came flying out of the stands to celebrate the touchdown and the bowl destination the Tigers earned.

"I remember thinking about playing for a national championship and having an opportunity to play on the stage that everybody desires to play on," said linebacker Jeff Davis. "Reflecting upon those things when the oranges came out, it hit home that we had accomplished something that hadn't been accomplished in a long time, and also what that meant, that that was going to give us an opportunity to win a national championship."

Clemson increased its lead to 15-7 by halftime, and tailback Chuck McSwain, Rod's brother, took over in the second half. Chuck McSwain usually alternated with Cliff Austin, but Austin was injured early in the second half. McSwain found that he missed Austin as the half wound down, and Clemson tried to run out the clock with the lead.

"I raised my hand many times to come out," McSwain said, "and they just ignored me. 'Leave him in there. He's been fussing about carries. Now he's going to get them.' So I just kept running."

McSwain rushed for a career-high 151 yards on 25 attempts. After USC drew within 15-13 on a pass from Gordon Beckham to Horace Smith, McSwain scored the game's final two touchdowns on runs of one and 23 yards.

"He had an opportunity to carry the ball the majority of the time, and it indicated what he could have done had he been the guy, just like Cliff," said running backs coach Chuck Reedy. "If they'd have carried it all the time, either one of those guys would have been a 1,200 or 1,300-yuard rusher."

Clemson won 29-13, finishing undefeated in the regular season for the third time in school history, and the first time since 1948. Defeating the in-state rival to do it made it sweeter.

"I can't think of a better way to finish a cake off than whipping those Gamecocks and putting that icing on top," Jeff Davis said. "It was fulfilling in many ways."

Though the Tigers' season was over, their journey to No. 1 still was incomplete. Clemson was ranked No. 2 behind undefeated Pittsburgh, which played its regular-season finale against Penn State over Thanksgiving weekend.

Many Clemson players didn't know much about Penn State aside from the fact that Joe Paterno was head coach. They have never pulled so hard for Penn State in their lives. The Nittany Lions had been No. 1 earlier in the season, but lost twice in October.

Pitt and Dan Marino led 14-0 early, but lost 48-14 to Todd Blackledge and Penn State. When the polls were released, Clemson was No. 1 for the first time in school history.

"We left for the holidays rated No. 2 and came back No. 1," said defensive end Bill Smith. "We weren't there watching it together as a team. But I promise you, we were all watching it."

Nebraska, Clemson's opponent in the Orange Bowl, was ranked No. 4 by the AP. Nonetheless, there was still a sense among Clemson's players that they had something to prove.

They thought the media and fans throughout the nation questioned them because they came from the traditionally weak ACC, and because they were playing an established national power.

"You knew the stars from Nebraska," said wide receiver Perry Tuttle. "You knew about Dave Rimington. You knew about [Mike] Rozier. Those players were getting a lot of press. ... We, on the other hand, the country bumpkins, tiger paw on the helmet, the people that believed in us were the people that drove from South Carolina. It wasn't the people from across the nation—it was the people from South Carolina."

9

ORANGE INVASION, MIAMI HEAT

" We were underdogs going into the game. We had a little chip on our shoulder because of that—ranked No. 1 and underdogs. I guess they thought they had the best big linemen and the big backs and all that kind of stuff; that they could just come in and run over us. But not with the defense we had. **"**

—Quarterback Homer Jordan

C lemson's Orange Bowl preparation began in New Smyrna Beach, where Danny Ford put the Tigers through a brutal barrage of drills. Ford's foresight with regard to conditioning proved a decisive factor in the game. On the night of the Orange Bowl, the temperature in Miami was 77 degrees, and the 74-percent humidity made it feel much warmer.

The Tigers' early trip to Florida helped them prepare for the heat. New Smyrna Beach was a small retirement community without much for the players to do, and they literally suffered at the hands of their coach. They didn't hit much. Many of the full-contact drills were saved for workouts that occurred later in Miami.

Instead, the Tigers ran. They ran 40-yard dashes, then ran through their drills at breakneck speed without pads. They ran until some of them were at the point of vomiting.

Under their breath, some players cursed the coach who had led them to an 11-0 record and the No. 1 ranking. Bowl games are supposed to be a reward for players, not a punishment, and these practices were torturous.

During pregame warmups, Clemson's players began to see the wisdom of Ford's preparation. Nose tackle William Devane looked over at the Nebraska players, who were warming up without their pads, and they were wringing, soaking wet with sweat. Clemson's players had pads on and were barely sweating.

The game hadn't even started, and the top-ranked underdogs from South Carolina were gaining confidence.

"That was a big, big warmup," Devane said.

Later, the players wanted to thank Ford for properly preparing them for the game. Defensive tackle Dan Benish lost 13 pounds in the Orange Bowl. Quarterback Homer Jordan fainted after the game.

The Nebraska players fared much worse. Benish remembers looking at Nebraska center Dave Rimington during the second quarter. By that time, Rimington could hardly catch his breath, and Benish and fellow defensive tackle Jeff Bryant felt great.

Nebraska wasn't as prepared for the heat because it waited until the official bowl week practices began in Miami to come to Florida. Nonetheless, the cocky Cornhuskers sneered at Clemson's players during bowl week, apparently believing that the smallish Tigers couldn't stand up to Nebraska because of its superior size and strength.

Before one pre-bowl event, Clemson's team bus arrived as Nebraska's was leaving. Nebraska positioned its biggest, strongest players outside its bus, and they snickered as Clemson's players walked past them. The Tigers fully admit they weren't nearly as big or strong as the Cornhuskers. It didn't matter. In this game, speed and stamina outpaced strength and bulk.

"They ran out of steam toward the end of the game," Benish said. "If they had been in shape, they might have been able to do something. But they couldn't come off the line. They couldn't do anything."

AGENTS OF ORANGE

The other thing that stood out about the New Smyrna Beach practices was the adoring support of the fans. It's well known that as many as 40,000 traveled to cheer the Tigers in the Orange Bowl. The late Clemson broadcaster Jim Phillips used to say some fans took out second mortgages on their homes or decided to forgo Christmas gifts that year in order to be present for a once-in-a-lifetime game. The amount of fans who showed up as the Tigers practiced in New Smyrna Beach was almost as impressive.

"There were fans there at practice," said cornerback Anthony Rose. "I can't remember a day, unless we had a closed practice, where we walked off the field and someone didn't ask for an autograph. Some of the fans were from that area, but some had traveled hundreds of miles to come down to support us."

With much of the hard work accomplished in New Smyrna Beach, Clemson's practices were a bit less intense in Miami—though they did have full contact in full pads. In New Smyrna Beach, the practices were so exhausting that they spent most of their free time sleeping.

They had more fun when they got to Miami. They made a trip to an alligator farm, and some of them ate a meal at the Playboy club. Another meal scheduled on a cruise ship was canceled because of a fire on board.

At the Orange Bowl parade, defensive tackle Ray Brown was awed as he looked at the famous Clydesdale horses. All this was new and fun for players who, for the most part, grew up in small towns in the South.

"I hadn't realized that they had air-conditioned trucks for those horses," Brown said. "They treated those horses like royalty."

The players were overwhelmed by fan support as they pulled up to the Orange Bowl on the team buses the evening of the game. Fans dressed in orange stood four and five deep, lining the streets of Miami, cheering the players and waving as the bus passed. It was dark already,

Danny Ford prepared his team for the heat in Miami with a brutal running regimen during practices in New Smyrna Beach.

and the stadium lights were on, and Benish said there was orange everywhere. It seemed as though every Clemson fan in the stadium came to the entrance to greet the team as the bus arrived. Benish saw the word "Orange Bowl" on the outside of the stadium, and thought how intimidating it would be for Nebraska's players when their bus arrived and they saw all the orange and only sparse pockets of red.

Clemson's players were so excited they were ready to come out of their skin.

"We had to wait all day, ready to play, and we pulled up to the stadium, and everything you could imagine was orange," Benish said. "It was orange signs, Tiger paws, bands playing. It was amazing. That victory, you could hand a piece of that to the fans, to us, the university. Everything was just perfect in that game."

That excitement boiled over during pregame warmups, as the players ran off so much nervous energy that defensive backs coach Curley Hallman began to worry.

Hallman didn't want the players to use up all their energy before the game and be sluggish when it started. He told them they were thoroughbreds, comparing them to horses in the Kentucky Derby. Often the horse that bucks wildly going into the gate is the last one to make the first turn because he exhausts himself before the race.

"You can't run the race before it starts," Hallman told the players. "You've got to slow it down."

The Rose Bowl game on NBC before the Orange Bowl lasted longer than expected, delaying the start of Clemson-Nebraska. Already nervous as they awaited the game they had waited a lifetime to play, Clemson's players got bad news from the official in the locker room following warmups. They would have to wait five or 10 minutes longer to take the field.

Ford told the players to take off their helmets and shoulder pads, because they were going to be there a while. Television monitors in the locker room showed the Rose Bowl. During a break, NBC cut away to promote the evening Orange Bowl broadcast. The camera showed the view from the Goodyear Blimp overhead, with the stadium lit brilliantly.

"This is it," punt returner Billy Davis thought in the locker room. "That's us."

The players sat in the locker room, nervous and tight. Then Ford spoke up. Defensive end Bill Smith said Ford motioned toward the big, "boom box" stereo near Terry Kinard in the locker room.

"TK," he said. "Does that thing work?"

Kinard said it did.

"Well, turn it on."

The locker room was filled with music. Players started dancing. Coaches were laughing. An uptight team relaxed.

"It was exactly what we needed five or 10 minutes before we were about to play the biggest game of our lives," Smith said.

RIMINGTON: CENTER OF ATTENTION

The key to Clemson's game plan defensively was controlling Nebraska's Dave Rimington, one of the best centers ever to play college football. He is the only two-time winner of the Outland Trophy as the nation's best interior lineman, having won in 1981 and 1982. The Rimington Trophy, given annually to the nation's best center, was named after him.

Rimington met his match in the Orange Bowl when he faced Clemson's nose tackle tandem of William Devane and William Perry. Theirs was a remarkable relationship, the 265-pound sophomore and the 285-pound freshman, both good enough to start.

Naturally, their competitive instincts made them want to play all the time, and there was talk of moving one of them to defensive tackle. But they decided the team would be better off if both played nose guard.

Perry served notice to Rimington that he wasn't going to back down from him during the week before the game. The teams attended a number of functions in Miami, including a Jai-Alai event where Perry spotted Rimington seated and watching the action.

"William Perry went down and sat in the seat right behind him," said Clemson place-kicker Bob Paulling. "Of course, William was a freshman, and everybody thought he was overrated and wasn't as phenomenal as he really was. It just kind of went from there."

In watching film of Rimington, defensive coordinator Tom Harper and defensive line coach Willie Anderson took note of Rimington's tendencies. Devane said that if ever there was a center who could have been accused of illegal procedure, it was Rimington. He was big, strong and quick, and he moved into the player he was blocking a split second before he snapped the ball. Rimington's perfect timing avoided detection by the officials but gained him an instant advantage at the line of scrimmage.

On the first play, Rimington got the best of Perry, driving him back five or 10 yards and disrupting the flow of Jeff Davis and the Clemson linebackers. In the huddle before the next play, Davis glared at Perry. Then, using Davis' nickname, Perry addressed him.

"Judge," he said. "That won't happen again."

For the rest of the game, Perry and Devane wore out Rimington. They took turns throwing their weight at him in hopes they would break his spirit.

"If you've got two guys pounding on that one guy, it made a huge difference," Devane said.

Ford also made a key adjustment especially for Rimington. His film study showed that Rimington—like many great offensive linemen—often got away with holding penalties. Ford made up his mind to discuss this with the officials before the game.

"They called holding on him twice that night," said Joe White, the Clemson academic advisor. "And one time, it was a very crucial situation."

Nebraska won the coin toss and chose to receive. Clemson chose to defend the east goal. Donald Igwebuike kicked off to Mike Rozier, the 1983 Heisman Trophy winner, who returned 18 yards up the middle before Craig Crawford brought him down.

The game was on.

"It was just the ultimate experience," said holder Anthony Parete. "You'd watched it so many times growing up that I couldn't imagine being there myself. ... I was awestruck."

Clemson's defense held Nebraska to 256 yards and 13 first downs in a 22-15 victory in the Orange Bowl.

TIGERS STRIKE FIRST

It didn't take long for Clemson's defense—ranked second in the nation in scoring after giving up 8.2 points per game—to assert itself. On the third play from scrimmage, Nebraska faced third-and-2.

The Tigers went into a short-yardage, goal-line defense, lining up Devane and Perry next to each other in the middle. Clemson had a slant called, and Devane got across the face of one of the offensive guards and into the backfield. Nebraska was running an option play, and linebacker Danny Triplett blew it up. Quarterback Mark Mauer was hit as he attempted to pitch to Roger Craig, and the ball squirted free.

"You just dive for it," Devane said. He did, and came up with perhaps the most famous fumble recovery in Clemson history at the Nebraska 28-yard line. The first play on offense was a pass to Bubba Diggs.

It was just a 3-yard pass, but Diggs was thrilled. The emotion of playing the biggest game of their lives on national TV was almost overwhelming for these players.

"I have to be honest with you. Personally, probably the first pass of the game, which I caught [was the highlight of the Orange Bowl]," Diggs said. "I got the first one, and I thought there might be five or six more coming my way."

Diggs caught one more pass, for seven yards in the third quarter that night. After Diggs' first reception, Cliff Austin ran seven yards for a first down at the Nebraska 18. The drive stalled after that when Jordan was sacked for a 9-yard loss on third-and-10, so Donald Igwebuike came on to kick a 41-yard field goal.

Clemson led 3-0, and the psychological lift was far more substantial than the three points the Tigers put up on the scoreboard. It would turn out that night that Nebraska wasn't as well prepared, well conditioned, or as fast as the Tigers. But the Cornhuskers were used to playing in big games such as this, and they were huge, frightening physical specimens.

Clemson's players lacked big-game experience and needed something to reassure them that their speed and conditioning could overwhelm a bigger Nebraska team. Scoring just three minutes and 11

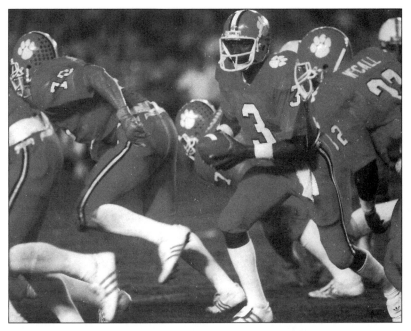

Quarterback Homer Jordan (3) was a gifted option runner and ranked 12th in the nation in passing efficiency in 1981.

seconds after kicking off to the Cornhuskers gave Clemson tremendous confidence.

"When we got out on the field and William Devane recovered that fumble on the third play, I think we all knew we could play with those guys," Benish said. "They were like everybody else. The big Nebraska Cornhuskers weren't anything different from anybody else."

The lead didn't hold up for long. Nebraska set up a big play by running Rozier four consecutive times to start the next drive. Clemson was penalized twice for illegal procedure, and then the Cornhuskers caught the Clemson defensive backs peeking into the backfield at Rozier. Anthony Steels got behind the defense, and Rozier hit him with a halfback pass for 25 yards and the game's first touchdown.

"[Terry] Kinard, who in my opinion is probably the best free safety who ever played in the ACC, came up thinking it was a run," said wide

Tailback Cliff Austin scored Clemson's first touchdown in the Orange Bowl on a 2-yard run.

receiver Perry Tuttle, "and the receiver snuck behind him, and it was a pass."

The Clemson defense was fooled badly on that play, but quickly atoned for the mistake. On Nebraska's next drive, safety Tim Childers caught Mauer for a loss of 11 yards, forcing the Cornhuskers to punt from their own 5-yard line.

Clemson took possession at the Nebraska 42-yard line and gained a first down when a Jordan pass for Jeff Stockstill resulted in a pass interference penalty. Igwebuike kicked a 37-yard field goal to cut the deficit to a point.

The Tiger offense made its first big play in the second quarter, when Jordan passed deep to Frank Magwood. Nebraska safety Sammy Sims tipped the ball.

"I kept my eyes on the ball the whole time it was in the air," Magwood said. "I saw the defender cut in front of me. He tried to make the interception. He tipped it, and I kept my concentration on the ball and made a good catch."

The gain was 42 yards to the Cornhusker 12-yard line, the longest play of the game from scrimmage. Two plays later, cornerback Ric Lindquist intercepted Jordan in the end zone; but this was largely a game of field position, so Magwood's catch remained important. Rozier fumbled when he was hit by Joe Glenn, and Jeff Davis recovered at the Nebraska 27.

On third-and-4 from the Nebraska 9, Clemson called timeout. The television broadcast team questioned offensive coordinator Nelson Stokley for the quarterback draw call coming out of that timeout, but Jordan scooted up the middle for four yards and a first down. Two plays later, Austin took a pitchout wide right for the touchdown. He had experienced perhaps the most difficult day of anybody on the team, and he didn't show up for one of his meetings with the running backs.

"When he wasn't there, we knew something was wrong," said running backs coach Chuck Reedy. "It didn't take long before we realized and found out what had happened."

Austin was stuck on an elevator at the hotel for about two hours. Reedy said the coaches worried about what effect that would have on Austin, but he was fine and rushed for 22 yards on seven carries.

Ford called for a two-point conversion attempt in hopes that Clemson could extend its lead to seven points. Jordan underthrew Tuttle, and Clemson led 12-7, an advantage it would take into halftime.

THIRD-QUARTER DOMINATION

The first half had been a chance to show the nation Clemson belonged on this stage, and the Tigers did by reaching halftime with a lead. In the third quarter, Clemson established itself as the dominating team in the game that would earn and deserve the national title.

Clemson's scoring drives had measured three, 21, and 27 yards in the first half as the defense did the heavy lifting. Overshadowed by the defense in many ways for much of the season, the offense made its mark in the third quarter with the game's biggest drive, though a holding penalty and clipping penalty forced an early Clemson punt.

Cornerback Anthony Rose nearly got the Tigers the ball back in Nebraska territory after Bill Smith tipped a Mauer pass at the line of scrimmage. The officials ruled that Rose trapped the ball against the ground and called the pass incomplete. Rose has always disputed that call.

"I caught it before it hit the ground," he protested. "Instant replay would have given it to us. It would have been overturned."

Instant replay review in college football officiating still was 24 years away, so Nebraska ran another play before being forced to punt by Clemson. The most critical drive of the game was about to start.

On first-and-10 at the Clemson 25, Jordan passed 12 yards to Tuttle. Another pass to Tuttle on third-and-5 was good for a first down and moved the ball into Nebraska territory at the 42. This would be Jordan's best drive, as he went 4-for-4 passing for 48 yards.

After Chuck McSwain ran nine yards to the Nebraska 16, the Cornhuskers called timeout, but they couldn't stop Clemson's momentum. Jeff McCall ran 12 yards up the middle for a first-and-goal at the 4.

McSwain tried the left side but gained just one yard. Clemson botched a pitchout to McSwain to the right for a loss of 10 yards, making it third-and-goal from the 13. Ahead 12-7, Clemson needed a touchdown. A field goal wouldn't have done a lot of good, because it would have given the Tigers an eight-point margin; and Nebraska could have tied with a touchdown and two-point conversion.

As Jordan came to the line of scrimmage, he saw Tuttle off to his left, covered man-to-man by cornerback Allen Lyday. Jordan nodded at Tuttle, wanting him to run a fade route.

"Name any receiver worth his game who wouldn't want to have man-to-man, one-on-one in a situation like that," Tuttle said. "He took the inside away, played inside just a little bit. Homer just threw a perfect

Clemson captain and middle linebacker Jeff Davis, right, made a team-high 14 tackles in the Orange Bowl. Teammate Andy Headen, center, knocked Nebraska's last-gasp pass to the turf.

strike, a great ball to catch, where it really screwed the defensive back in the ground. He kind of lost a sense of where the ball was coming from."

Tuttle soon would be immortalized on Clemson's only cover in the history of *Sports Illustrated*, triumphantly holding the ball after that catch. It was his school-record eighth touchdown reception of the season, and it capped a 12-play, 75-yard drive. The Tigers led 19-7 and were beginning to pull away from the Cornhuskers, who couldn't get anything going on offense.

Nebraska's offense was like Clemson's, dependent on a strong rushing attack with Rozier and Craig to wear down opposing defenses. But the Tigers weren't wearing down because Nebraska couldn't get first downs to keep them on the field.

Clemson forced another punt, and punt returner Billy Davis responded with the biggest special teams play of the day. Davis always wondered whether Clemson's names for its punt return schemes were wise. The call for a return to the left was "orange," which was okay. But a right return was "white," and as Davis came onto the field shouting "white," he thought the opponents would think he was yelling "right" and be tipped off to Clemson's plan.

If Nebraska knew the plan on this "white" return, it didn't make a difference. Davis fielded Grant Campbell's punt cleanly and got good blocks from Randy Cheek and Jimmy Scott.

"I broke a tackle, and, wow, I was out in the open," Davis said. "Then you just run like a scalded dog, as fast as you could go."

After Davis' 42-yard return earlier in the season at North Carolina, defensive backs coach Curley Hallman took him aside and told him that if he had cut to the middle instead of the sideline, he would have scored. Davis said Hallman's advice might have been on his mind as he cut into the middle in the Orange Bowl.

Now people tell Davis all the time that he would have scored on his return in the Orange Bowl if he would have cut to the sideline. Instead, Irving Fryar caught him at the Nebraska 22 after a 47-yard return. Davis believes he probably would have gotten his picture in *Sports Illustrated* if he had scored to increase the lead to 26-7.

"I wouldn't change a thing," Davis said. "I wouldn't go back for a minute and say I'd rather have a touchdown. I'll take a 47-yard return. I wouldn't change a thing, because you never know what would happen. All that matters is that we fought them off till the end."

A holding penalty took Clemson back to the fringe of field goal range, but Jordan passed 16 yards to Jerry Gaillard. On third-and-3 from the 15, Jordan ran wide left but was tackled for a 5-yard loss. Igwebuike kicked his third field goal of the game, a 36-yarder, and the Tigers led 22-7 with 2:36 remaining in the third quarter.

After Jeff Davis barely missed intercepting a Mauer pass early in the fourth quarter, Nebraska came to life. Rozier ran for eight and nine yards, then appeared ready to attempt a halfback pass and scrambled up the middle instead for an 8-yard gain.

"Rozier with his high knees, it was just fun to watch," Tuttle said. "Even when I was on the sideline and the defensive team was on the field, I was such a spectator that game."

Rozier ran 12 yards up the middle, and then Craig scooted around the left end for a 26-yard gain and a touchdown with 9:15 remaining.

The Cornhuskers had been down 15 points, so they needed two touchdowns with a two-point conversion after each to win by one because there was no overtime in college football. Nebraska was penalized five yards for delay of game and was forced to go eight yards for the conversion.

Mauer called an audible to a running play that went right into the teeth of a Clemson blitz. Craig took a pitchout to the left, shed a tackler, and ran in for two.

"I'll never forget Tom Osborne coming out on the field," said Clemson academic coordinator Joe White, who watched from the sideline. "You could just tell he was getting all over the quarterback [for calling the audible]. Then he just sort of hit him on the head as if to say, 'Good call.'"

TIGERS HANG ON

Clemson had to nurse a seven-point lead for what seemed like an eternity. Tuttle made the mistake of bringing the ball out from two yards deep in the end zone, and only got to the 12-yard line. After three plays gained just one yard, it appeared that Nebraska was going to get the ball in fantastic field position.

Dale Hatcher, one of college football's best punters ever, didn't let that happen. He boomed a 50-yard punt that was fair caught by Fryar at the Nebraska 37-yard line. The Cornhuskers went right back to Rozier, who zipped up the middle to midfield before Jeff Bryant brought him down. Clemson caught a break, though, when Nebraska was called for holding. It was first-and-14, and on third-and-4 two plays later, Mauer went down for a loss of three yards just before making an errant pitch to Craig.

Nebraska punted, and a Clemson offense built just for this situation took over at its 20 with 5:24 remaining. All the time Danny Ford spent building a punishing rushing attack and all the painful conditioning Clemson did in New Smyrna Beach was going to pay off—right here.

The Tigers needed their offensive line to blow Nebraska off the ball so they could keep the ball on the ground and not risk an incomplete pass that would stop the clock. Fullback Jeff McCall got the call three straight times, delivering a precious first down with a four-yard gain on third-and-3.

Clemson had three more downs to run more time off the clock. It was time for Jordan to deliver perhaps the greatest clutch performance ever seen by Clemson in a bowl game. A player with less heart probably wouldn't have even been on the field.

"At halftime, they didn't know if he was going to be able to play the second half," said reserve quarterback Anthony Parete. "I just remember him being exhausted."

This is where Jordan's recollection of the game diverges from those of his teammates and coaches, most likely out of modesty. Ford called it one of the most courageous efforts he had ever seen, because Jordan truly gave every ounce of his energy to the game and the team. Quarterbacks coach and offensive coordinator Nelson Stokely said Jordan was a special young man who burned himself out at the end of that game. Jordan makes no such claim. On third-and-4 from the Clemson 37, Jordan carried to his right on a keeper, then cut back to the middle of the field. Ford said he's still not sure how Jordan squirted free, but he did. He ran 21 yards to the Nebraska 40 for a first down that would allow the Tigers to keep the ball and run more time off the clock.

"I didn't know it was that big of a deal, really," Jordan said. "I was so tired. I laid there for a while. One of the guys kind of came and helped me up. People start talking about, it was the one that sealed the game. But I just ran the ball, and they told me to hang onto the ball, and I hung onto the ball. I just ran a little sprintout and just kept it and happened to pick up a couple of yards."

That's how Jordan tells the story. During the postgame revelry in the locker room, Reedy looked for Jordan and couldn't find him. He learned that Jordan was with the team trainers and set out to find him.

Years later, Reedy told the story about what he found to motivate his players when he was head coach at Baylor. Jordan was packed in ice,

Center Jeff Lytton raises his helmet in triumph at the Orange Bowl.

with an IV in his arm. The team physician, Dr. Byron Harder, was at his side. Reedy asked what was wrong.

"He's completely dehydrated," Dr. Harder told Reedy. "If he'd had one more snap to play, he wouldn't have made it. He gave it everything he had."

Clemson took a delay-of-game penalty, trying to milk every precious second off the clock. After a McCall gain of one yard, Nebraska took its final timeout. Just 1:43 remained. Jordan ran for four yards on second down, and then McSwain took a pitchout and gained one yard up the middle.

Rather than risk a blocked punt on fourth down, the Clemson staff instructed Jordan to run it again. He lost two yards, and Nebraska took possession with six seconds remaining at its own 46-yard line.

Benish had been sitting on the bench near the end of the Orange Bowl while Jordan worked his magic. Benish watched the clock as it wound down inside four minutes, three minutes, two minutes.

He wanted the seconds to tick away quickly so that Clemson's championship season could be complete. At the same time, he wished he could hold onto those sweet moments forever. He never wanted them to end.

"I remember thinking to myself, 'I've got to remember this in my mind, because it's going to be something I'll never want to forget,'" Benish said. "And it was true."

THE FINAL ACT

Benish and the defense took the field as Nebraska had time for one final, desperate play.

Clemson was in its dime coverage with safety Billy Davis deep and Kinard deeper to prevent a long, freak touchdown as Mauer lofted a pass for Todd Brown. Davis saw the ball coming straight for him, and linebacker Andy Headen got to it first and knocked it to the turf, a former quarterback taking unparalleled joy in causing an incompletion.

Cameras were everywhere as Ford rode on the shoulders of a sea of players out to midfield. Billy Davis said the Clemson fans cheered wildly in the end zone as he ran off the field. Players were throwing chin straps and pads into the stands to give the fans mementos.

"What can you say?" Davis said. "It was the ultimate thrill to be able to pull that off for those people."

Some fans showed their appreciation by getting memorabilia down to the players. One fan was wearing a giant, orange cowboy hat and tossed it Frisbee-style down to place-kicker Bob Paulling, who still has that hat.

Though there was concern for Jordan because he had to be rehydrated intravenously following the game, the players danced and shouted and embraced as they came to grips with the incredible accomplishment of finishing the season undefeated.

Kinard was approached on the field by a fan who offered him $100 for his jersey. Kinard might not have been able to keep his jersey after the season was over, but there's no telling how much money it would be worth now as a collector's item.

Clemson backup cornerback Vandell Arrington (1) celebrates the national title on the field at the Orange Bowl.

"Dummy," Kinard said. "I wish I had it now. I said, 'One hundred dollars? For this thing here? You can have it.'"

Kinard still occasionally watches the videotape of NBC's broadcast of the Orange Bowl. One of his favorite moments is from the end of the broadcast, after the Tigers have won and are filing into the locker room.

"I see myself coming in, and the expression, the big smile on my face, and I'm happy we won that football game," Kinard said. "That was it. The high we were on, I don't think we came down for weeks. It just was a happy time."

Said Devane: "Once we got back in the locker room, it was almost pandemonium."

There was a hospitality room open for Clemson back at the hotel after the game.

"Guys and girls," Clemson staff members and their families were told, "we're open as long as you want to stay."

Some of them stayed all night. This was a once-in-a-lifetime event for many of the people in that room, and they were going to enjoy it.

At that time, the Orange Bowl held its banquet the day after the game. It was a downer for Nebraska's players and coaches to have to stay an extra day after losing, but Clemson's players—though tired— enjoyed it.

That evening, one of the greatest games in the history of NFL football was held in the Orange Bowl. The Miami Dolphins and San Diego Chargers took their turn in the draining heat and humidity, with the Chargers winning the playoff game 41-38. Chargers tight end Kellen Winslow caught 13 passes for 166 yards despite being nearly as drained as Homer Jordan was the previous night.

"I always liked San Diego for some reason, and I got scolded pretty good," said Paulling, who was watching on TV. "Of course we were in the middle of Miami ... so I had to pipe down a little bit."

The coaches from Clemson and Nebraska exchanged kind words at the banquet and developed a friendship at the Orange Bowl. Nebraska's players were bigger and stronger, and Clemson's players won because they were faster and in better shape, but the teams were more similar than different.

Both played physical defense, enjoyed dominating opponents with power football behind tough offensive linemen, and ran the option. It's common for coaches to visit different schools during spring practice to get new ideas, and Clemson's coaches visited Nebraska that spring following the Orange Bowl.

Reedy said Nebraska coach Tom Osborne told the Clemson coaches that no crowd had ever flustered the Cornhuskers until that game. Nebraska fully expected to encounter hostile fans at Oklahoma and was prepared for them there. They didn't have any idea how many Clemson fans would flood the Orange Bowl for the biggest game in their school's history. They were intimidated because they hadn't anticipated such a hostile crowd at a supposedly neutral site.

"It was a phenomenal statement for him to make, but I think he was right," Reedy said. "The crowd had a tremendous impact on that game."

10

AFTERMATH:
Stories from 1981 and Beyond

"If you look at the lives of the gentlemen on that team, you will see that they have sought more victories. Yes, the national championship was something that happened in our lives, but we no longer dwell on it. Our actions say that we won it, and we're looking to win others. **"**

—Linebacker Jeff Davis

P resident Ronald Reagan noticed the cowboy boots Jerry Gaillard was wearing with his suit and tie at the White House. Reagan pulled Gaillard aside and remarked that he had a pair of boots exactly like Gaillard's.

"President Reagan was as normal a person as you or I," Gaillard said.

One of the best perks for any national championship team is the opportunity to visit the White House. Clemson selected wide receiver Gaillard and quarterback Homer Jordan to represent the team and the school in Washington, D.C.

While Senator Strom Thurmond looks on, wide receiver Jerry Gaillard meets President Ronald Reagan at the White House.

It was a cold weekend, and travel was bumpy on the little four-seat school planes that carried Jordan, Gaillard, and school officials to Washington. Grateful to arrive in Washington, the Clemson contingent found Senator Strom Thurmond eager to serve as host for the Tigers. Politicians at various functions asked what the Orange Bowl was like. At the White House, Gaillard sat at the desk in the Oval Office and was photographed pretending he was signing some important document.

Clemson's players brought President Reagan a football and a six-pack of specially packaged orange soda to commemorate the visit. When presented with the football, Reagan told the players that they couldn't throw the football into the stands when he played because they used one ball for the entire game. President Reagan spent about 20 minutes with the Clemson folks, more than Gaillard expected.

"Getting chosen to represent the University and the team was a real milestone," Gaillard said proudly.

DAVIS' SECRET SERVICE

The first thing Billy Davis saw when he walked into the late Senator Strom Thurmond's office on Capitol Hill was the football, on a pedestal, under glass.

It was a game ball from the Orange Bowl, signed by members of Clemson's national championship team.

"Clemson 22, Nebraska 15," it read. "National champions."

Clemson promotions director Allison Dalton had arranged for Davis to interview with Thurmond on Capitol Hill after Davis completed his undergraduate work following a short NFL career.

Davis first met Augustine Tantillo, Thurmond's chief of staff and a Clemson graduate. Davis told Tantillo that Thurmond certainly wouldn't remember him, but had shaken his hand in the locker room after the Tigers defeated Maryland to clinch the ACC title in 1981.

When recounting one of his most memorable conversations ever, Davis uses a low, gravelly voice to mimic Thurmond.

Thurmond showed Davis the ball from the Orange Bowl.

"Mr. Davis, were you on this team?"

"Yes, sir."

"Did you play in this game?"

"I sure did."

"Well, come on in here and talk to me."

Davis got the job and started working in Thurmond's mail room. Later, Thurmond made Davis his personal assistant.

"This is Mr. Davis," Thurmond would say when introducing him. "He used to play football at Clemson."

Thurmond would hit Davis in the chest.

"He looks like he still could," Thurmond would cackle.

Davis went on to work in the Secret Service. He served on Arkansas governor Bill Clinton's protection detail when Clinton ran for president and spent five years protecting Clinton after he became president.

Later, Davis traveled to 44 foreign countries in five years, worked as a Secret Service liaison to Capitol Hill and protected L. Paul Bremer, who was administrator of the U.S.-led occupation of Iraq.

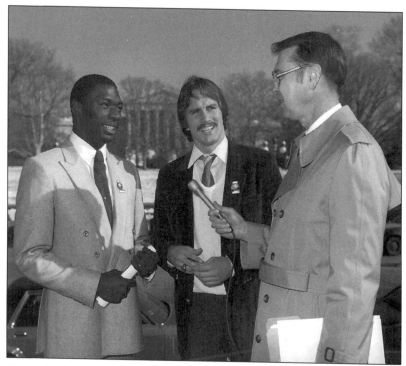

Quarterback Homer Jordan, left, and wide receiver Jerry Gaillard represented the team in Washington, D.C., when the Tigers were honored by President Ronald Reagan.

He moved to Atlanta in July of 2005 and spent each home game day in 2005 on the Clemson sideline because he finally was close enough to campus to spend more time at the school.

"Sometimes I'm at a loss for words," Davis said. "I try to think about how lucky and blessed I've been to do it. As a kid, you think about what you would like to do. Play college football. Then play in the NFL. Then, how about be a Secret Service agent?"

Despite doing all those incredible things in his life, Davis said he would work for free for Clemson if given the chance. His answer to a question on the Secret Service exam illustrated his appreciation for his experience on Clemson's national championship football team.

He was asked to name the three people he most admired, besides his parents.

Davis named Ronald Reagan, Strom Thurmond, and Danny Ford.

ROAD TRIPPING

Some of the most pleasant memories for the players of their time at Clemson came from the ways they entertained themselves when they barely had two nickels to rub together.

Football fans remember Terry Kinard as one of the greatest free safeties ever to play college football. Tight end Bubba Diggs remembers Kinard as the roommate who was constantly tinkering with his Volkswagen. Kinard bought the Volkswagen after Diggs was in a crash that ruined Kinard's orange Datsun. The Volkswagen was nothing but trouble.

Diggs and Kinard were visiting friends in Columbia one time when a snowstorm hit. They were snowed in for a day or two, then tried to crank the Volkswagen when it was time to leave. All the oil had leaked out of the car, and it took $700 worth of repairs to get it moving again.

Kinard said the car was never right after those repairs. The accelerator cable broke often, and the car would break into a fast idle when that happened. Kinard would drive anyway, often slowing down to 10 miles per hour going up a hill and speeding up to 80 miles per hour going down. Applying the brakes was about the only way to control the car's speed.

"It was just burning up brakes," Diggs said.

Kinard also had problems getting the car started because of a carburetor problem. When he went home to Sumter for a weekend, the car would sit idle for two days and would be extremely difficult to start afterward. When Kinard was ready to go back to Clemson, he would gather family members to help. They would push the car up and down the street while Kinard attempted to start it.

When it finally got started, Kinard waved good-bye and continued on his way. Kinard chuckled recently as he recalled the hardships of growing up a poor college student.

"What we lived on was the basic necessities," Kinard said. "We didn't have anything extravagant. Times were hard, and when I went to Clemson on a scholarship, that's probably the only way I would have been able to go."

When they had free time, Kinard and Diggs loved to get in the car and just drive to different areas of South Carolina. When a short circuit prevented the Volkswagen's headlights from coming on, they made sure they did all their traveling during daylight hours.

Diggs said they had gas money and not much else.

"We used to take some of the corn flakes out of the cafeteria two or three days a week, so we would have something to snack on at night," Diggs said. "I'm telling you, we did what we had to do, and it was an absolute blast, and I mean that in every sense of the word."

Dan Benish tells a similar story of road tripping with his roommate, Danny Triplett. Benish, who grew up in Hubbard, Ohio, had never been to the ocean before. They piled into Triplett's Datsun with about $40 between them and headed to Myrtle Beach. They spent three days there.

"We had enough to put gas in the car and buy a case of beer," Benish said.

What more could a college student need?

NCAA FALLOUT

When the team bus pulled up to Williams-Brice Stadium in 1981, fans of Clemson's rival, South Carolina, held up signs taunting the Tigers.

"It's probation time again," punt returner Billy Davis remembers reading on one of the signs.

Davis said players wondered what those Gamecock fans knew that the Clemson players didn't know. Some of the players were so busy practicing and keeping up with their schoolwork that they had no idea the NCAA was investigating Clemson. They didn't have time to read the newspaper reports about two high school players from Knoxville, Tennessee, who accused Clemson's staff of violations.

According to a *Philadelphia Daily News* report, the high school players—James Cofer and Terry Minor—claimed on ABC-TV that Clemson's coaches gave them about $1,500 in an effort to get them to attend Clemson.

The players and coaches who saw or heard about the ABC report were incensed. Some charged that ABC used the story to discredit Clemson in the hopes that the ratings would suffer for the Orange Bowl on rival network NBC. That seems a dubious accusation. If anything, the hint of scandal made Clemson a more interesting television commodity.

"I thought we were doing it all the right way, but when you beat some of these people, and they're not used to losing to you, they came after you pretty good," said athletics director Bill McLellan.

It wasn't until November 22, 1982, that the NCAA finally released its infractions report. The violations were significant in number and severity. Members of the coaching staff and boosters were cited. Violations included the offer of a substantial amount of cash and an automobile; an offer to pay for two sisters of a prospect to attend Clemson; and the awarding of a scholarship to the friend of a prospect.

Clemson was put on probation for two years, which kept the school out of bowl games and off live television. In an old-fashioned display of Clemson ingenuity, McLellan made the best of the situation by contracting with fledgling all-sports network ESPN and USA to carry the Tigers on tape delay.

"The year(s) that we were restricted from TV, it was live TV, and it didn't say anything about delayed TV," McLellan said. "I got exposure for every one of the games."

The players on the championship team don't dispute that the violations occurred or that they were gravely serious. Still, they were deeply upset by the pall cast over them by probation.

Friends sometimes ask Billy Davis if he cheers for Clemson's ACC brethren when the Tigers aren't playing. He said he doesn't.

"I still have a raw taste in my mouth for the conference," Davis said. "They stuck it to us. They gave us another year [of probation, beyond the NCAA's two]. I venture to say if it was North Carolina or anybody else, they wouldn't have done that. That's kind of a Tobacco Road conspiracy theory we have in the Palmetto State."

Davis and his mother, Shirley Davis, laugh when people talk about Clemson as a renegade, cheating program because of the probation. They remember that during the recruiting process, Clemson didn't offer Davis any extra inducements, though other schools Davis won't name did.

If Clemson was regularly giving cash, cars or both to recruits, Davis figures, he would have been near the top of the list for impermissible payments. He was the top-rated recruit in the state of Virginia. He was important enough that, when he was taken to an off-campus party on his official visit, Steve Fuller and Dwight Clark greeted him at the door and made sure he felt comfortable.

Davis' family income was so modest that his mother and sister, Jenny, slept on the dorm room floor of Davis' friend, Heather Herndon, when they visited campus. They piled in the car for the trip from Alexandria, Virgina, to Clemson with baloney sandwiches and mustard to eat on the trip.

"My parents couldn't even afford to get a hotel room," Davis said. "It's a joke. People were saying, 'You guys were paid. They're paying your way.' My folks would be lucky when we left to give me five dollars for me to go to McDonald's. Then you hear all this stuff about how we cheated."

TIGER TALES

Inside the Tiger mascot outfit, Ricky Capps couldn't believe it when Chuck McSwain ran 12 yards for Clemson's 10th touchdown in the third quarter against Wake Forest.

Just 61 seconds earlier, Perry Tuttle had scored the Tigers' ninth touchdown on a 25-yard pass from Homer Jordan. Any Clemson fan knows the Tiger is required to do push-ups equal to Clemson's total points on the scoreboard every time Clemson scores.

Tuttle's touchdown gave Clemson 62 points.

"Before I completed the 62 push-ups for the 62nd point, the team had already scored again, and I had to do 69 more," Capps said.

Capps played basketball and pole vaulted in high school before becoming a member of Clemson's junior varsity cheerleading squad as a freshman. When he was a junior in 1980, Capps began a two-year stint as the Tiger. As he prepared to run down the hill to enter Memorial Stadium with the team, peering at the cheering crowd through two holes in the Tiger's nose, Capps felt transformed.

"All of a sudden you become the symbol of Clemson University," Capps said. "All of a sudden, you're not you. You're the Tiger."

The 1981 season was eventful for Capps. He still has a picture of himself, exhausted, with the head of the Tiger costume at his side after working the Wofford game with temperatures in the mid-80s.

Then there was the Wake Forest game. After the Tiger did the 69 push-ups for McSwain's score, Duke Holloman ran three yards for a fourth-quarter touchdown. The Demon Deacon mascot came over and graciously offered to do 76 push-ups.

Capps accepted.

"The Clemson faithful, they absolutely loved that—the sportsmanship involved in it," Capps said.

Capps did his own push-ups after Craig Crawford ran 72 yards for Clemson's final touchdown as the Tigers won 82-24. Capps finished the day with 465 push-ups, a school-mascot record that still stands, but it was hardly his only adventure that season.

He was riding in full uniform on his motorcycle to a pep rally one Friday when he had to downshift going up a hill near the president's house.

When he did, a cape his mother had made for him—with a Tiger paw on the back and an "S" for "SuperTiger" on the front—got caught in the spokes. The bike flipped over about six times.

"Into the ditch I went," Capps said. "About 25 people thought they had lost the Tiger."

The Tiger escaped with cuts, bumps, and bruises. When Clemson traveled to North Carolina for the first meeting between top-10 teams in ACC history, he had to protect his tail. A radio station host in North Carolina called to tell him a fraternity in Chapel Hill had offered a

$100 bounty for anybody who could take the tail off the Tiger and bring it to the fraternity house.

Capps said there was no way anyone was getting that tail. The radio host called back to say the reward was increased to $250 after the fraternity brothers heard Capps' defiant interview. A day later, the reward increased to $500.

"Being a poor college student, for $500, I may tear the tail off the Tiger suit and bring it to you myself," Capps replied.

He resisted that temptation. During the game, fans in the stands made four or five attempts to steal the Tiger's tail. Clemson's cheerleaders acted as a security squad to protect Capps.

The Tiger kept its tail, and the bounty went unclaimed.

After the Orange Bowl, though, Capps gladly gave the head of the Tiger to coach Danny Ford when they met by chance in a parking garage. Ford put on the Tiger head and posed for photographs.

"It was a long time ago, but to Clemson people, it seems like yesterday," Capps said. "It was unreal to be involved in that, and for the team to be crowned the national champion."

SUPERSTITIOUS MINDS

After Clemson won its first few games, defensive backs coach Curley Hallman began to notice that players were becoming superstitious.

"We were on that roll where you can tell those kids are believing they can't be beaten," Hallman said. "When you do that, and I've been on some other teams that are the same way, they always sit in the same chair. Everything has to be the same."

Many players say they didn't have any superstitions, but others did. Place-kicker Bob Paulling's brother-in-law, Ricky Rucker, attended the first few games wearing an old, straw hat.

As the season went on, the "lucky hat" was a necessity every week.

"By the end of the season it was all torn up," Paulling said. "He wore it anyway. We won 11 games, and that old straw hat was all beat up."

When Clemson played in the Orange Bowl, Rucker was there—with his straw hat on his head.

Hallman liked to make his Thursday meetings with the defensive backs relaxed that season. His wife, Barbara, would bake chocolate chip cookies for him to take to the players, and he would serve Cokes to them. They would enjoy their refreshments while they watched film and reviewed assignments before practice.

One Thursday late in the season, Hallman forgot the cookies. Barbara had baked them, but Hallman left them at home. He walked in the meeting and didn't think anything of it. All the players were in their customary seats as he walked toward the chalkboard.

He never got there. Free safety Terry Kinard—Hallman called him "Bruiser"—asked if he was forgetting something.

"We're not going to have this meeting," Kinard said.

Hallman asked what was wrong.

"Coach," Kinard replied, "where are our cookies and our Cokes?"

Explaining that he had forgotten the cookies, Hallman said he'd get the players their cookies after practice. Their superstitions wouldn't allow that.

"We need them," Kinard said. "Right now."

Fortunately, Hallman lived about two miles from campus. He hustled home, fetched the cookies, and got back to campus in time to feed the players and continue with the meeting.

"Terry wasn't going to let anything change," Hallman said.

MAMA SCOTT

After tight end Bubba Diggs had emergency surgery to remove his ruptured spleen, his parents came from his home in Augusta, Georgia, to care for him.

When it was clear that Diggs was going to be okay, Dora Scott of Pendleton said she would care for him until he was ready to return to his dorm.

"I was like her adopted son," Diggs said. "That's one lady who, if it wasn't for her, I don't know if I would have made it."

Scott's daughter, Layneigh, was a student at Clemson and brought home friends—young men, women, and sometimes football players—to her childhood home on Route 187 about a mile from Pendleton

High School. There, "Mama Scott" as the students called Dora, hosted them for meals and made sure they went to church on Sundays. Scott lost her husband in Vietnam in 1965.

"I never married again," Scott said. "I stayed home and raised my daughters and took care of my parents. It just meant so much to me to have those boys at my house."

Diggs, Jeff Davis, Perry Tuttle, and others attended services at New Holly Life Baptist Church on Sunday mornings with Scott. They were called the "salt-and-pepper boys" in the congregation because black students and white students all came together at Scott's urging.

About 15 of them formed a choir group called the "Singing Tigers" and sang at the church. After church was over on Sunday afternoons, they would go to Scott's house for lunch. She served baked and fried chicken, macaroni and cheese, collard greens, broccoli and rice casserole. The players returned her kindness by helping her look after her 1 1/2 -acre yard.

Scott grew to love them. She was sitting in the second row at the Gator Bowl when Charlie Bauman, whom Scott called one of "her boys," was slugged by Ohio State coach Woody Hayes in 1979.

"It was terrible," Scott said. "You know how bad mama was hurting? I'd rather for them to hit me than one of my boys."

Players' families were grateful their sons had a place to go occasionally for a home-cooked meal and church services. Some parents didn't have money to stay in a hotel when they visited campus, and Scott welcomed them into her home or arranged for them to stay with friends.

Scott, who was 43 when Clemson won the Orange Bowl, even told some of the students who came to visit where she left the keys on her back patio.

"It's not that way anymore," Scott said. "You can't do that now. You can't do any of that now."

Scott longs for the bygone days when she could leave her door unlocked at night and welcome people who were nearly strangers into her house without fear. Her daughter is a counselor for their church, so she brings home the children she works with now instead of Clemson students.

Many of the students Scott fed and entertained still visit regularly. Diggs, one of her favorites, calls at least twice a month just to check up on her. Scott said her friends make sure her yard is well maintained and her health is good.

"I know I'll never end up in a rest home," she said. "I'll always have somebody to take care of me."

SUPER TIGERS

Dan Benish can't get his national championship ring on his finger anymore because he was thinner when he received it than he is now.

He also earned a ring from Super Bowl XXII, when he helped the Washington Redskins defeat Denver 42-10 at the end of the 1987 season to become NFL champions. He doesn't hesitate when asked which championship meant more to him. The Super Bowl was all about business and getting to the top of his profession. The national championship was an accomplishment for a bunch of lifelong friends.

"We're bonded for life," Benish said. "Everybody has the utmost respect for each other, it doesn't matter if we were starters or backup players or even scout team players. I've got 50 or 60 guys there that I can say are friends of mine for the rest of my life. That's the most special thing."

Benish was the last of the four players from the 1981 team to win a Super Bowl. William Perry won as a rookie in the 1985 season, when he became a cultural phenomenon as a defensive tackle and goal line fullback on Mike Ditka's Chicago Bears team. Perry scored a touchdown on a 1-yard run in the Bears' 46-10 romp over New England in Super Bowl XX.

Safety Terry Kinard and linebacker Andy Headen helped the New York Giants defeat the Denver Broncos 39-20 to win Super Bowl XXI at the conclusion of the 1986 season. Kinard said what set the national championship season apart was the appreciation of Clemson's fans. The Giants won another Super Bowl just four years after Kinard's team won. Clemson has never won another national title.

"They appreciate what we did back then because they see how hard it is to repeat it, to stay at that level, play at that level, be able to win that championship because it's been over 20-some years now," Kinard said.

The NFL success of players from the 1981 team is a good barometer of its talent and the recruiting of Danny Ford and Charley Pell before him. Though some Clemson opponents—Georgia, Nebraska, even North Carolina—were reputed to have more talent than the Tigers, Clemson proved to have more than its share of tremendous athletes. Eighteen members of the 1981 team made NFL rosters. Four—Kinard, punter Dale Hatcher, running back Kevin Mack and linebacker Johnny Rembert—made the Pro Bowl. Kinard, Mack, Perry, Hatcher, and Jeff Bryant all made NFL all-rookie teams, and Hatcher led the NFL in net punting in 1985.

Billy Davis, who played a year for the St. Louis Cardinals in the NFL, said resentment at being overlooked fueled the careers of many Clemson players.

"What makes us special, we're a small school in the northwest corner of a small state, and we use that as a chip on our shoulder in a conference where everybody looks down on us," Davis said. "Everybody still looks down on us. It's Clemson. It's the cow college."

Safety Tim Childers said that, because Clemson didn't have a national reputation, people underestimated its talent. The "Cinderella story" angle gets played up more because the Tigers were unranked in the preseason, coming off a 6-5 season and played for a school that was unfamiliar to many fans before 1981.

In a way that does the 1981 team a disservice.

"To this day, I don't think people look at that team and look at the level of ability and talent on that team," Childers said. "From the defensive side, a lot of those guys went on to play at the next level, and that was the nucleus of our team."

CHAMPIONSHIP ATTITUDE

After the Augusta Stallions announced that they were starting an arena football team in his hometown, Bubba Diggs told his wife he was going to apply for a job as an assistant coach. She told him to forget it because he had never played or coached arena football.

"Football is football," he said, and he went to the interview with head coach Mike Neu armed with two powerful items.

Neu noticed his Orange Bowl and national championship rings, and Diggs took them off so Neu could see them. Diggs explained that he hadn't coached arena football, but said it didn't make a difference.

"I am a winner," he told Neu. "I've got a winning attitude. I know how to win—three conference championships, one national championship."

When he was through selling himself, Diggs said, he would have been shocked if Neu didn't hire him. He got the job and coached arena football for a few years until the travel got to be too much for him and his young family.

His Clemson connections helped him many times throughout his life. He was driving from Augusta to Aiken for William Perry's wedding, where Diggs was scheduled to be the best man, when a South Carolina highway patrolman pulled him over for speeding.

Diggs was wearing a Clemson shirt, and the trooper asked him what he was doing. When he explained that he was going to Perry's wedding, the trooper said he would void the ticket and give him a warning—on one condition. The trooper asked him to get Perry's autograph on the ticket and told him where he would be the next day when Diggs was driving home. Diggs got Perry to sign, and, still dressed in his tuxedo, found the trooper the next day.

"He was cool, man, and we both laughed about it, though I've never seen him again," Diggs said. "That was one of the wildest things."

Diggs' national championship profile hasn't gotten him out of every jam, though. After he was selected by the Washington Federals in the short-lived United States Football League's territorial draft, he left Clemson and drove home on South Carolina-Route 28.

He was wearing Clemson gear this time, too, when he was pulled over for speeding.

"How about them Tigers," Diggs said hopefully.

"How about 'em?" the officer answered. "Go Cocks."

The officer gave Diggs his ticket and told him where to mail his check to pay the fine.

'PEOPLE SAY THEY REMEMBER'

Even more than 20 years after the Tigers won the national title, former players and coaches are astounded by the attention they get for their participation on the national championship team.

Larry Van Der Heyden, who lives in Clemson and coached the offensive line, retired from coaching in June of 2005 and began substitute teaching that fall just to keep busy. He couldn't believe how many middle school students came up to him and asked him about his coaching days—specifically about the 1981 team.

Wide receiver Frank Magwood attended the Clemson-Miami game at Death Valley in 2005 and was approached by an alumnus who attended school during the early 1980s. Magwood was a good player and doesn't look much different now than he did then, but he's hardly the most famous player from that team. The guy still recognized him.

"People always respect the players from that team," Magwood said. "That's something that won't ever go away. Everywhere you go, even now, people say they remember me from the championship team."

Members of that team are split, though, on whether the national champions are afforded the proper amount of respect by the school and a generation of young people born long after the Tigers won the national title whose only exposure to it is word of mouth. Tailback Chuck McSwain said he is proud to see "1981 National Champions" displayed on the scoreboard at Death Valley. Van Der Heyden wonders why the display can't be more prominent.

Van Der Heyden said the students he meets as a substitute teacher are so interested in hearing about the national title, he needs to remember to bring his championship ring to school one day to show them.

Terry Kinard has a different experience with the high school players he coaches near his home in an Atlanta suburb. He said they are aware of the heights he reached in football, but couldn't care less.

Coach Danny Ford poses with the Orange Bowl trophy. He said Bear Bryant, his coach at Alabama, brought him up to expect to win at the highest level.

"These kids, they don't think about that kind of stuff," Kinard said. "That stuff doesn't do anything for them, actually. The one thing I stay away from is talking about me and what I did."

Kinard said his pupils don't even watch much college or pro football during their free time anymore. They are more interested in playing video games.

When he comes to Clemson, though, Kinard said people always recognize him and congratulate him on winning the title.

"They talk about those days, the days back when we played, and how much they appreciate that we won the national championship," Kinard said. "The fans, the people, they appreciate the way we played back then, because we played some pretty good football."

EPILOGUE

❝ I wear it every day. I wear the Orange Bowl ring as well as the national championship ring. I can have bad days but I can just look down on my ring and reflect and remember. It wasn't all glory or good. It was blood, sweat, and tears. I mean that. **❞**

—Tight end Bubba Diggs

It's impossible to imagine what Clemson might be like if the 1981 team hadn't won the national championship.

Many people throughout the country had never heard of Clemson before the Orange Bowl meeting with Nebraska. On NBC's broadcast of the game, a graphic showed a map pinpointing Clemson's location for those who weren't aware.

"That was a significant thing to put Clemson on the map as far as a dominant school for football," said defensive end Ray Brown.

Any college administrator will tell you that exposure for the entire university is one of the most desirable benefits of a successful athletic program. The unfortunate reality is that while research and education are the missions of a university, the lab and the classroom don't make for compelling television.

Each time the Clemson football team appears on national television, the name recognition the school gets is priceless. That's why in some cases schools or their conferences pay "sponsorships" to the bowls they attend. The exposure is worth the price they pay, and not just for football recruiting.

The national championship also helped Clemson people believe in themselves.

"It showed the people at Clemson that we can be successful," said defensive end Bill Smith. "Even though we're small, even though we're tucked up in the foothills of the mountains of South Carolina, if we put our minds to it, we can be successful, whatever it is, whether it's athletics, academics, whatever."

Smith has been a member of Clemson's board of trustees since 1996. He joined the board out of love for the school, because he wanted to give back to the university that means so much to him.

He said that during the 1980s, some people did know Clemson just for its national title and the success it had in bowl games against Penn State, Oklahoma, and other teams. But he said Clemson's academic reputation has been boosted dramatically in recent years.

"Now it's more of a good blend of academic success and athletic success," Smith said, "and people are starting to recognize Clemson not just in this country but around the world."

As the years pass and Clemson has yet to return to a major bowl game, let alone play for a national title, the significance of that season has increased. On one hand, Clemson fans hold that season up as an example of what the school should and can do in football.

Clemson coach Tommy Bowden says the job is attractive because the school has won a national title. On the other hand, without a huge natural population base from which to draw recruits, the school is at a disadvantage compared to perennial powers such as Texas, Southern California and the Sunshine State trio of Florida, Florida State, and Miami.

"It's something we should shoot for every year," punt returner Billy Davis said of Clemson and the national title, "but if we don't win it, it's not like it's not a successful season. We don't have the recruiting base of Florida State. We don't have South Beach to sell like Miami. We don't have Atlanta to sell like Georgia Tech."

Nonetheless, Davis remains convinced Clemson can become a national champion again. There is optimism among others involved with the 1981 championship team that the Tigers will rule college football again some time:

"You want your school to win and get some more," tailback Chuck McSwain said hopefully.

"I think Clemson can win another national championship," defensive backs coach Curley Hallman said. "I really do. There are certain things in place there. When you bring prospects in, they like that atmosphere."

"Certainly Clemson will win another one at some point in time," said wide receivers coach Lawson Holland.

The 25 years that have elapsed are enough that some of the young men Clemson recruits are unaware that the Tigers have won a national title. Billy Davis was at an event with 1981 teammate Reid Ingle when David Pollack, the former Georgia defensive end, noticed Ingle's ring.

Pollack asked Ingle what it was.

Ingle told him it was his national championship ring.

"I didn't know Clemson won a national championship," replied Pollack—who was recruited heavily by the Clemson staff.

Nonetheless, the 1981 season's effect on the entire university is obvious to anyone who spends significant time on campus.

Clemson president James Barker's goal is to make the school a top-20 public university. In its rankings of public universities for 2006, *U.S. News & World Report* had Clemson No. 34. It's impossible to tell whether this would have happened without the athletics success whose pinnacle was the 1981 national championship, because it's impossible to imagine the school minus the most significant national event in its history.

The championship certainly didn't hurt.

"We showed people that if you believe in yourself, you can accomplish whatever you want to," Smith said. "Whether it's faculty or administration or whatever, if you think you can be a top-20 institution, it can all work together and you will be there."

Celebrate the Variety of Carolina Sports
in These Other Recent Releases from Sports Publishing!